LYRICS FOR FREEDOM;

AND

OTHER POEMS.

UNDER THE AUSPICES OF THE CONTINENTAL CLUB.

NEW YORK:
Carleton, Publisher, 413 *Broadway.*
(Late Rudd & Carleton.)
M DCCC LXII.

WYNKOOP, HALLENBECK & THOMAS,
Printers,
No. 113 Fulton Street, New York.

INTRODUCTION.

At a regular meeting of the Continental Club, held at their rooms, April 25th, 1862, the President, on taking the chair, said:

"*Gentlemen*—Before proceeding with the regular business of the Club, I wish to invite your consideration to a very novel request, entirely unprecedented in the annals of our venerable society." (At these words of the President, the members of the Club, expecting something of rare interest, at once became very attentive.) "Some of the younger members of the Club have, in an exuberance of patriotism, composed several poems on the present convulsions of the Commonwealth. I have not read them, but they are, by our learned Secretary, said to be good, bad, and indifferent. The novel request of the authors of these poems is, that permission be granted to have them published under the auspices of the Continental Club. This, gentlemen, I frankly tell you, I am opposed to. If the Club should step beyond the limits of its hitherto well-observed propriety, to entertain such a startling innovation upon its ancient character, it would certainly betray a lack of dignity, that I am unwilling to sanction. In deference, however, to the wishes of some of my fellow-members, I have presented the subject to you for your action." After a short discussion, chiefly among the older members, who were more afraid of the dignity of the venerable society being infringed than of any positive harm from the proposed publication, the Secretary announced the decision of the Club :—"That these Poems should be published UNDER THE AUSPICES OF THE CONTINENTAL CLUB."

CONTENTS.

HYMNS TO THE REPUBLIC: PAGE

The Commonwealth, 3

The Rising of the North, 9

Columbia Needs no Heraldry, 13

Let Freedom's Banner Stream, 15

Men of the Clime where Liberty, 18

Columbia! Queen of the West, 21

God Bless the Brave Old Flag, 23

The Republic's Rehabilitation, 25

THE BATTLE-FIELD:

The Field of Glory, 29

Battle of the Cumberland, 34

Sigel's Charge, 42

Battle of Shiloh, 46

PICTURES OF THE WAR:

PAGE

War's Compensation, - - - - - - - - - - - - - 53
Let it Toll! Let it Toll! - - - - - - - - - - - 56
The Sorrow-stricken Vale, - - - - - - - - - - - 58
Nuptial Dirge, - - - - - - - - - - - - - - - - 62
The Dying Soldier, - - - - - - - - - - - - - - 65
Twilight's Gloom, - - - - - - - - - - - - - - - 69
Martial Dirge, - - - - - - - - - - - - - - - - 72

HOME AND CAMP:

A Soldier's Life for Me, - - - - - - - - - - - 77
Adieu, - 80
The Soldier Lover's Dream, - - - - - - - - - - 82
Oh, Annie! wilt thou walk with me? - - - - - - 84
Song, - 86
It Breaks at Last, - - - - - - - - - - - - - - 88

SHRINE OF THE BRAVE:

Ambition, - - - - - - - - - - - - - - - - - - - 93
The Mausoleum of the Brave, - - - - - - - - - 95
Love's Pilgrimage, - - - - - - - - - - - - - - 100

SHADOWS OF DESTINY: PAGE

Oh, Lightly Lies the Head at Night, - - - - - 109
Hope's Guerdon, - - - - - - - - - - - - - - - 111
Halting in the Breach, - - - - - - - - - - - - 115
The Shadow of Nemesis, - - - - - - - - - - - 117
The Fall of Feudalism, - - - - - - - - - - - 120

LYRICS FOR FREEDOM:

The Song of Labor, - - - - - - - - - - - - - 131
The Patriot's Prayer, - - - - - - - - - - - - 133
The Tax-payer's Song, - - - - - - - - - - - - 140
Two or Three Millions of Dollars a Day, - - - 146
Knocking them Down, - - - - - - - - - - - - 149

AMONG THE LOWLY:

The Cabin Door, - - - - - - - - - - - - - - 159
Under the Pine-tree's Shade, - - - - - - - - 163

TO ENGLAND, THESE:

A Homely Epistle from Brother Jonathan to John Bull, - - - - - - - - - - - - - - - - - - 167
The Meteor Flag of England, - - - - - - - - - 178

PASQUINADES:

PAGE

King Cotton and King Corn, - - - - - - - - - - 185

Natural History of the Lion, - - - - - - - - - 193

A Word to Jeff, - - - - - - - - - - - - - - 197

John Bull sends a Missionary to the American Cannibals, - - - - - - - - - - - - - - - - - 200

The Battle of Newbern; or, Chivalry on the Rampage, - - - - - - - - - - - - - - - - 203

About a Piece of Cheese, - - - - - - - - - - - 208

An Old Joke Newly Versified, - - - - - - - - - 209

Government Officers Reporting to the President, 210

Biblical Authority for Rebellion, - - - - - - 211

The Anaconda, - - - - - - - - - - - - - - - - 213

My Chivalry! Good Night! - - - - - - - - - - 214

The Herculean Plan, - - - - - - - - - - - - - 216

Nursery Rhymes, - - - - - - - - - - - - - - - 217

The Mudsills, - - - - - - - - - - - - - - - - 218

Sambo's View, - - - - - - - - - - - - - - - - 219

Sapere aude:
Incipe. Vivendi recte qui prorogat horam,
Rusticus expectat dum defluat amnis ; at ille
Labitur et labetur in omne volubilis ævum.

—Horace.

Sic volvenda ætas commutat tempora rerum :
Quod fuit in pretio, fit nullo denique honore ;
Porro aliud succedit, et e contemptibus exit,
Inque dies magis appetitur, floretque repertum
Laudibus, et miro est mortales inter honore.

—Lucretius.

PRELUDE.

Why should we sing? Was ever Song
Allied with the cause of Wrong?
Poesy's immortal shell
Has sung the woes of Man so well,
It has become the potent charm
To shield the weak from tyrant's harm.

To those who brave, on every field,
Oppression's hosts with sturdy shield,
She grants the guerdon of her power,
To aid the struggle of the hour:
Shrin'd within their hearts alway,
Like prow of Hope against the spray.

Where'er the weak, by power crush'd,
Their moaning cries in dungeons hush'd,
And the cold world's indifference
Sneers at their vain impotence,
The soul of Song their agony
Embalms in one eternal cry!

And gathering thus, as ages roll,
Till, like the wind, from pole to pole,
It sweeps with unimpeded force,
While Retribution marks its course,
And only stays its fell career
When all avenged is every tear.

What foul Oppression wrung from those,
Bow'd to earth with weight of woes,
Till all aveng'd the life-long pain
Of bruiséd limb and fever'd brain:
And they whose family ties were torn
The image of one God had worn!

Higher yet the song shall rise,
Till angels sing it in the skies ;
And yet its mournful burden bear,
Though hallowed in that heavenly air ;
Though sweetened much by pure incense,
With all its aim the more intense.

How man, far worse than murderous Cain,
Had bound his mate with festering chain.
Had made the victim of his lust,
Creatures made of equal dust ;
Had parted hearts, he would not know
Had broken by the cruel blow !

How e'en Religion cloaked the Wrong ;—
Then swelled the climax of the song.
God's love to all on earth was given,
To light them on their way to Heaven ;
And falls with rich equality
Upon the bondman and the free.

The Lord is just; his vengeance dire
Flashes like a sword of fire!
The iron chains of thousand years
Asunder in a moment tears.
Then will the terror-stricken horde
Sink beneath the avenging sword!

Then should we sing, when woes like these,
To tell them o'er, the blood would freeze,
Like ghosts still hang upon our track,
And keep our march of greatness back;
Oh! that from our shield were torn
The sign that makes us food for scorn!

Yes! let the noblest throbs of Song
Be ever rais'd against the Wrong!
And who shall say what heavenly light
Shall shine adown the gloomy night,
And, as the rays of morn increase,
Set seal upon eternal peace!

Hymns to the Republic.

REMEMBER, Oh my friends, the laws, the rights,
The generous plan of power deliver'd down,
From age to age, by your renown'd forefathers,
(So dearly bought, the price of so much blood.)
Oh, let it never perish in your hands!
But piously transmit it to your children.
Do thou, great Liberty, inspire our souls,
And make our lives in thy possession happy,
Or our deaths glorious in thy just defense.

—ADDISON.

THE COMMONWEALTH.

CLIME of the West! young Freedom's rugged home
Was slowly reared upon thy savage breast.
The wind's wild music and the billows' foam
Startled thine eagle from his rocky nest
Upon thy sea-girt coast, as if possessed
Of ardor such as those who freely gave
Their starried ensign, emblem of the West,
In Heaven's ethereal airs to brightly wave,
And Freedom win beneath, or welcome Honor's grave!

Spirits of that stormy time! Glory's wreaths
Were never twined for nobler brows than yours;
Above your tombs the soul of Freedom breathes
Immortal fame; and e'en on other shores,
Where thy genius, Liberty, seldom soars,
Where regal masters rule, a tyrant horde—
The fettered slave his prayer in secret pours,
For Heaven to grant such men to draw his sword,
And proud defiance hurl against his feudal lord.

Herculean labors stared ye in the face;
But these increased the nerve to stem the strife
For Liberty and Justice. Lived one so base
To bargain honor for that poor thing, life?
Who would not gladly greet the warring knife,
If, dying thus, he could bequeath a name
To time unsullied, alone with virtue rife?
Alas! there have been such; their country's shame!
But they can never live in Virtue's cherished fame.

Blessed by approving Heaven, the altar rose,
And Glory came, her choicest wreaths to twine;
Then, like receding waves, rolled back her foes.
Devoted hearts attended near the shrine,
Winning a niche in Fame's illustrious line,
While Freedom's stars came twinkling one by one,
And settled 'round that spirit, half divine;
Then her flag beamed and glittered in the sun,
As millions blessed the worth — the deeds of WASHINGTON.

Great man! thy life hath left to hist'ry's page
The purest record of thy country's fame!
In vain we praise the heroes of an age;
Like the autumnal leaves, before thy name,
They crumble into dust. They cannot claim
One laureled leaf, which 'round thy noble brow
The past hath girt; the future still the same;
Revolving years will to thy deeds bestow
Their meed of just applause, that adds a brighter glow.

Thy noble heritage in time became
The vampire's spoil; sucking the life-blood dry,
So that its soul, all pandered unto shame,
In fortune's sun might for the moment lie,
Then, like the venom'd serpent, loathsomely
Crawl through its slimy ooze unto the dust,
Which shall at last conceal it from the eye
That saw with grief the heavy, blighting rust
Gnawing the nation's life, with foul, insatiate lust.

Glory shall float above Columbia's crest
With grandeur's pride and pomp, as never yet
She soared above the nations, East or West.
Brighter than o'er Saladin's minaret;
Than where the Adriatic's breakers fret
The fallen wave-wed city's rotten quays,
Thy sun arose, as if 'twould never set;
For, though grand, those were but Oppression's days,
That hung, like heavy nights, o'er Freedom's struggling rays!

Thy beams shall light the Commonwealth anew,
Upon the path that godlike heroes tread,
And ever to her mission steadfast, true,
Behold in time her brows all garlanded
By thy angel, that has her footsteps led
To this high seat, where in honored state
Of kingly mummery she sits instead.
From Freedom's travail, though it comes but late,
Shall spring the glorious fruit that makes the nation great.

As truth immortal, the unshackled mind,
With richer than Indian pearls inlaid,
Shall soar aloft, free as the mountain wind,
Where Freedom's form of beauty is displayed!
Never of worldly contumely afraid,
Its onward course, majestic and serene,
Like the proud sun, that never is delayed
When passing clouds of darkness intervene,
Sweeps down unto its couch in Glory's dazzling sheen.

The centuried oak braves the winter's shock,
Wrestling like a stout giant with the foe,
And lifts its arms in triumph o'er the rock,
'Gainst which in vain the torrents dash below.
So lofty mind heeds not the maddening flow
Of passion at its feet, for upward lies
The path of duty. If the tempests blow,
Still through the storm, with trusting, faithful eyes,
Waiteth with patient hope for Freedom's cloudless skies.

And think you not such cloudless skies shall come?
Or must we of our heritage be shorn?
To admonitions of the past be dumb,
And, powerless, behold our 'scutcheon torn
By those who have its fortune's favors worn?
Or shall the honest heart and willing hand
Lead forth in beauty, like the blushing morn
Sweeps the Orient with her jocund band,
Fair Freedom as the hope of this distracted land?

THE RISING OF THE NORTH.

LIKE giant from repose,
The mighty North arose,
To battle with the foes
On the hearth,
That warmed the serpent's length,
Till gath'ring all its strength,
With foul, envenomed tongue
The breast that saved it stung;
That bore the rankling thorn,
That made her name the scorn
Of the earth.

Swift as Aurora's horn
Awakens joyous morn,
A million men seemed born
With her breath!
So fleetly rushed they forth,
From East, and West, and North.
To defend the heritage,
Won in heroic age;
'Gainst England's stern array,
They won the battle fray
At the death!

The spirit of the Lord
Gleams like a fiery sword,
Smiting the trait'rous horde
In his wrath!
Whose all-sufficient light
Scatters the clouds of night;
And, like a faithful star,
The fortunes of the war
Guides with prayerful song,
The mighty hosts along
Freedom's path.

What sturdy knights are these,
Swift as the mountain breeze,
Firm as their native trees,
In the fight?
When drum to trumpet spoke,
They stood with hearts of oak,
Against the battle's swell,
While comrades round them fell;
Bearing on every field
That sign upon their shield—
"God and Right!"

Crowned with wreaths of glory,
Their names will live in story,
While youth, and manhood hoary,
Hymn their praise!
When round the winter fire,
Their children to inspire,
To emulate the deeds
That sowed our Freedom's seeds,
With tearful eye and cheek,
The sire and matron speak
Of these days.

With Freedom's flag unfurled,
If need be, 'gainst the world,
Though envy's shafts be hurled
At her breast:
By her people's gallant arm,
And with Freedom's magic charm,
The stars upon her shrine
With splendor still shall shine,
Upon the land and sea,
The beacons of the free
In the West!

COLUMBIA NEEDS NO HERALDRY.

Columbia needs no heraldry,
  Nor strange time-honored crest,
To stamp her name and title clear,
  The queen of all the West!
The stars of Heaven upon her shield
  In silver clusters shine;
The wreaths of fame that bind her brows,
  Her thankful millions twine.

From sea to sea her cities spread,
  While fields of golden grain,
And thriving villages, give note
  Of Freedom's prosperous reign.
While swiftly, at her trumpet call,
  From mountain, wood and glen,
To battle in her righteous cause,
  Come troops of sturdy men.

And though rebel foes assault,
  Her legions could withstand
A world in arms, when battling for
  Their honored native land!
And, through the clouds that darken now,
  The morning soon shall come;
And Peace, with Plenty in her train,
  Displace the martial drum!

LET FREEDOM'S BANNER STREAM.

LET Freedom's starry banner stream
  Proudly against the northern sky!
Lighting, with Heaven's reflected beam,
  A trusting people's heart and eye!

Firm as the steadfast Northern Star,
  That guides the sailor on the deep,
Twill wave above the fields of war,
  A sign that Freedom still doth keep

Her watchful vigils o'er the land,
  On which this heavy night doth press;
And will reveal, at God's command,
  The glory of her loveliness!

Her spirit still on wings of love,
  Though sorrow floats upon her plume,
Winnows our country's clime above,
  Till happier days shall all illume.

She is not dead, but surely wakes,
  As sunlit day shall follow night;
And when her morning proudly breaks,
  The world will bless her flood of light!

When Empire o'er the mighty West
  The splendor of her pomp displays,
Fair Freedom, from her mountain crest,
  Shall lead the nation on its ways.

Then let the banner breast the gale,
  That ne'er again on flood or field
Shall float above a people's wail,
  But be their ever faithful shield!

MEN OF THE CLIME WHERE LIBERTY.

MEN of the clime where Liberty
  Has reared her starry crest—
A beacon light to all the world—
  A welcome to her breast:
Whose flag has waved o'er Freedom's soil,
  And e'en o'er Slavery's, too,
This foul rebellion rends in twain
  That glorious field of blue!
And shall the stars, that shone of yore
  Like Heaven's immortal light,
Ne'er gleam again, the sign of hope
  And promise in the night?

Shall sacrilegious hand be laid
  On Freedom's vestal shrine,
And crumble down the sturdy oak
  That shields the poisoned vine,
That long has tried to blast its strength,
  Ere comes that certain frost,
That leaves the gallant oak unharmed,
  While the parasite is lost?
Palsied be the hand that's raised
  Against that sacred tree,
Whose spreading boughs in time will shade
  No people but the free!

And when the wheeling car of Time
  A thousand years has rolled,
And with his funeral bell the fate
  Of countless nations tolled;
How they who ruled with arrogance
  And pomp the present hour,

Had passed and scarcely left a trace
  Of all their splendid power;
His brazen throat will ever peal
  The glories of thy past;
And shrine thy Freedom still untouched
  While Time itself shall last!

COLUMBIA! QUEEN OF THE WEST.

THE splendor of the Western Queen,
  Enthroned upon a continent,
A wondering world has never seen,
  Since Rome was hailed omnipotent.
Although she sits on either sea,
The bulwarks of her Liberty,
Her throne is in her people's breast—
Columbia! Queen of the West!

She needs no glory of the past
  To make her name an honored one!
Oppression's victims, gathering fast,
  To seek the protection of her sun,
Whose genial rays, alike on all,
Like Heaven's choicest blessings, fall,
Proclaim the noblest and the best—
Columbia! Queen of the West!

If in her mission she should fail,
  Her Freedom's beacon light grow dim,
The world, with an eternal wail,
  Would chant in weeds her funeral hymn!
Believe it not; it cannot be!
Still shall the shrine of Liberty
Upon thy soil in safety rest—
Columbia! Queen of the West!

GOD BLESS THE BRAVE OLD FLAG ![1]

"God bless the brave old Union flag!"
 Peals forth the choral strain.
The eye is gladdened with the sight—
 The heart leaps up again!

No keener joy felt Israel,
 When, in the wilderness,
They saw the faithful, promised sign,
 That ended their distress.

The dusky slaves with wondering eyes
Upon that banner gaze,
And smile to think its lustrous light
Their Freedom's path betrays!

The suffering brethren of our heart
Shed tears of joy, like rain;
And feel that, through that bitter night,
Their prayers were not in vain.

God bless the brave old Union flag!
That bids their sorrows cease;
Above whose folds the breaking light
Displays the bow of Peace!

THE REPUBLIC'S REHABILITATION.

WHEN the clouds of Rebellion arose in the West,
The spirit of Freedom came down from her crest;
Her bosom all anguish, her cheek all in tears,
For the stars that in madness had shot from their
spheres!

The arms of her people were eaten with rust;
And the flag of her glory was dragged in the dust;
And the clamor of rebels grew loud at her gate;
While the world sneered in scorn at the Common-
wealth's fate!

Then 'rose, like the whirlwind, at Freedom's alarm,
A million of men with invincible arm;
And rolled back in triumph the conquering tide,
And planted their banner again in its pride!

And the hosts of Rebellion all melted away,
Like the mists of the night at the coming of day;
And the spirit of Freedom has laid by the sword,
That triumphed in war by the help of the Lord.

The widows and orphans have stifled their grief:
In the fame of their loved ones have found their relief.
And a generous people will shield to their grave
The kindred of heroes so gallant and brave.

And the horrors of warfare alone were revealed,
Where Rebellion had blighted the husbandman's field.
And the Nation again on its mission of peace,
The stars of her glory shall never decrease!

The Battle Field.

Let them come;
They come like sacrifices in their trim,
And to the fire-ey'd maid of smoky war,
All hot, and bleeding, will we offer them:
The mailed Mars shall on his altar sit,
Up to the ears in blood. I am on fire,
To hear this rich reprisal is so nigh,
And yet not ours.

—King Henry IV.

THE FIELD OF GLORY.

The surging stream of battle
   Goes roaring down the plain,
'Mid the thunder and the rattle
   Of the bullet-driving rain.
Heart and pulse beat quicker ;
   No cheek is blanched with fear ;
The husky voice grows thicker,
   As they dash away a tear.

They do not fear the foeman—
  For the cry is, "Let him come!"
But a man will weep like woman
  When he thinks of those at home!
    Banners soaring;
    Cannons roaring;
    Ride o'er the dying;
    Charge the flying;
        Charge, charge, charge!

Is this the field of glory,
  Where the young and gallant dead
Live only in the story
  Of the battle where they bled?
None shall weep above them,
  As they blacken with the earth;
Those who long have loved them
  Will miss them from the hearth.

They die and are forgotten,
While the gen'ral bears the palm;
Then Fame is somewhat rotten,
And Honor's but a sham!
Banners soaring;
Cannons roaring;
Ride o'er the dying;
Charge the flying;
Charge, charge, charge!

Yes! 'tis a gallant sight,
To lead those hosts along,
In splendor and in might,
While rings the battle-song.
But breaks the dream of glory
When the smoke has cleared away;
When all that splendor's gory,
And those hosts are vultures' prey!

All-glorious are wars!
  Fade widows' tears away!
Honorable the scars
  Of soldiers in the fray!
    Banners soaring;
    Cannons roaring;
    Ride o'er the dying;
    Charge the flying;
        Charge, charge, charge!

Come to the field of battle!
  Come where the eagles soar!
List to the chill death-rattle,
  As the soldier gasps no more!
Look o'er the sickening plain:
  So much youth gone to death!
Look at the heaps of ghastly slain,
  And in horror hold your breath!

Is there above no Power
  To look on deeds like these,
And blast them in the hour
  Of their foul atrocities?
Yes! The immutable laws
  Of God rise above the glare
And glory of all that battle was:
  Man's punishment is there—
Upon that field of glory,
  Where the young and gallant dead,
Live only in the story
  Of the battle where they bled!
    Banners soaring;
    Cannons roaring;
    Ride o'er the dying;
    Charge the flying;
        Charge, charge, charge!

BATTLE OF THE CUMBERLAND. (2)

THE mighty hosts are gathering in the valley of
 the West,
Beneath their country's banner, with its star-illu-
 mined crest,
To fight the good fight of the free, where'er its
 folds may fly,
With GOD AND RIGHT upon their shield, and their
 good battle-cry.
The weeping sire and matron bless their only, gal-
 lant son,
And pray that, even with his life, the battle may
 be won!
The lovers plight again their troth, and with the
 sad adieu,

She bids him faithful be unto that starry field of
blue.
From peaceful fields and happy homes, these heroes
sally forth,
To fight the honest battle of the long-forbearing
North.
From Ohio's verdant valley to Indiana's plain ;
From Illinois' and Michigan's rich fields of waving
grain ;
Where Mississippi's rolling tide from icy fountains
breaks ;
From Wisconsin and from Iowa, unto the farthest
lakes ;
From Kansas' and Missouri's fields, unto Nebraska
wild,
Where Nature, in her grandest mood, her savage
rocks has piled ;
From the farms of Minnesota to the plains of
Tennessee—
From the "dark and bloody ground,"* again the
battle of the free

* Kentucky.

To fight with willing hearts and hands, three hundred thousand men
Bear down upon the dragon till they brave it in its den.

Oh, they little recked the glory or the grandeur of their cause,
They only knew that traitors foul had trampled on all laws;
And rashly raised the standard of Rebellion in the land,
Because the nation ceased to cringe to Slavery's iron hand.
Oh, they little recked the splendor of the conquest they might make,
But battled, like good faithful knights, for vestal Freedom's sake!
They remembered childhood's lessons, in that far New England home,
Ere through the Western prairies as pilgrims did they roam.

How they learned to lisp their little prayers, beside their mother's knee,
Whose bible taught them that the Lord had made all people free.
So went they forth, all panoplied with honor, to the fight,
And prayed unto the Lord of Hosts to guide their steps aright.

Oh, never, since the Saviour cleared the temple of the Lord
Of an impious race, who have been and will ever be abhorred,
To battle for the dearest rights, it's, oh, there never was,
For gallant knight to gird his loins, a more ennobling cause.
Like the waves upon the ocean, ere they break upon the shore,
You could hear the gathering of those hosts in long and sullen roar;

Till, slowly rolling up their strength, they dash
upon the rock,
And make a wreck of everything that braves their
thunder shock!
Or, like the fierce tornado, when it sweeps with
sudden wrath,
The slaughter of their enemies betrayed their vic-
tor path.
But, only on the field of war their prowess could
be seen,
For Peace and Plenty smiled again, wherever they
had been.
Their flag was like a Saviour to a terror-stricken
land,
That smiled again, in rosy light, like touch of
magic wand.

'Twas a splendid sight to see them, in their glori-
ous array,
Bear down, where in its leagured walls Rebellion
stood at bay.

And through the gloomy days and nights, like iron
heroes stand,
Because they knew the Lord would hold each life
within his hand.
Around the walls of raging fire, the gallant heroes
press,
The number of their noble band each moment grow-
ing less;
The sulphurous clouds have darkened all the canopy
of heaven,
And only breaks like ebon night with thunder-
clap is riven.
Along the valley, surging now, the bleeding waves
of war,
While belching fire of hundred guns seems shrink-
ing earth to jar.
And still, amid the din of arms, amid the fire and
smoke,
Those serried ranks of freemen ne'er from their
column broke;

But braved the deadly iron hail unto the 'leaguered walls,
And hand to hand in combat closed, until the rampart falls.
And, as Aurora's blushing train swept through the rosy east,
The morning light shone down upon a truly ghastly feast!
Like the leaves of yellow Autumn, that mighty host lay strewn,
And o'er the scene the angel Death in triumph rode alone!

Though the glory of the conquest was with the gallant West,
They saw the carnage 'round them there with sorely aching breast;
The truly great do always weep, e'en when the meanest fall,

And stoop, as to a holy task, to wind their funeral
pall!
But swiftly, as the mountain breeze, from field to
field they sweep,
Till the harvest of their glory leaves nothing more
to reap.

SIGEL'S CHARGE. (3)

ADOWN the tangled forest
  The rebel columns sweep;
While the thunder of artillery
  Is roaring loud and deep.
They laugh to see the little band
  Their onward tide oppose;
But quail before the leaden rain,
  And valor of their foes.

Throughout that long and dreary night
  Those gallant heroes stand;
Though 'round them close on every side
  Rebellion's savage band.
Full well they know, when morning breaks,
  The carnage will begin;
And desperate must their struggle be,
  If they the battle win.

Along the ridges and the vales,
  Broke forth no morning sun;
But o'er the gathering hosts of war
  The canopy was dun.
As if the morning sky was hung
  In weeds of solemn black,
For loyal youth whose death would pave
  The victors' gory track!

Bearing down, like fierce tornado,
  The savage rangers speed;
Their shout arose like demons' yell
  Above each dashing steed.
And the bravest held their breath,
  As that fearful war-cry broke;
When from the belching cannon loud
  The murderous volley spoke.

What, ho! my stout artilleryman!
  Why stand ye here alone,
Before your brazen cannon's throat,
  When all your mates have gone?
As foemen on that hero press,
  His fatal bullets peal;—
Oh, never sank on glory's field
  A heart more brave and leal!

Undaunted still the rangers rode,
 Straight through the fiery hell;
Though 'neath their feet in gory piles
 Their dying comrades fell.
Now, down upon these desperate men—
 'Mid sulphurous fire and smoke!
Who madly fight, but reel in death,
 Beneath our sabres' stroke!

As the reaper with his sickle
 Lays the harvest in its pride,
So in heaps those gallant rangers
 Were stricken by our side.
And fell in slaughtered groups along
 The victors' scathing way:
But gave the richest glory
 To our arms upon that day!

BATTLE OF SHILOH.

As th' East was streaked with light,
They burst upon our sight,
Keen for the eertain fight—
Rebellion's firm array.
In wild confusion then
Gathered our doomėd men,
While cannon from the glen
Broke on the morning gray.

Like wildered men who stand
Upon the moor's low sand,
While 'round on every hand
  Surges their warning roar:
Their shrieks of wild despair
Heeds not the gusty air;
But, lapping their matted hair,
  The breakers dash the shore!

Back to the river's brink—
Back where the cowards slink;—
Oh, must our banner sink
  Before yon brutal soldiery?
Is there no arm to save
The struggles of the brave?
Oh, will yon crimson wave
  Sweep all the Western chivalry?

Beneath their shot and shell
Our slaughtered soldiers fell,
While o'er them rose the yell
  Of drunken victory.
Oh, that the night would fall
Like Heaven's shield 'round all,
Or droop like mourning pall
  O'er Death's wild revelry!

But when the morning broke,
Reeled they beneath the stroke
(Like lightning-shivered oak)
  Of our cannon thundering!
Back with their squadrons then—
Won we the field again—
Our heaps of wounded men—
  But not again blundering!

Who won these garlands red,
Plucked from the gory bed
Of our dying and our dead,
  Should wear his ghastly glory!
While they who stemmed the tide,
Fast falling side by side,
Ever be their country's pride,—
  And immortal live in story.

Pictures of the War.

THEN, through the silence overhead,
An angel with a trumpet said,
"For evermore, for evermore,
The reign of violence is o'er!"
And, like an instrument that flings
Its music on another's strings,
The trumpet of the angel cast
Upon the heavenly lyre its blast,
And on from sphere to sphere the words
Re-echoed down the burning chords,—
"For evermore, for evermore,
The reign of violence is o'er!"

—LONGFELLOW.

WAR'S COMPENSATION.

SHADES of the Past, invoking shades to be!
(And, oh! may man here learn to hate ye more,
Viewing the woes ye give Humanity!)
Red and bloated War, stiff with crimson gore,
With clank of steel, the wide field rattles o'er.
Close on the monarch's step his subjects wait,
Hell's furies breathing from their every pore—
The spirits dread that rule delusive fate,
And prove the awful bane of many a conquered state.

Despair, gaunt-visaged, in her weeds arrayed,
While Moloch thunders from the field afar,
And Murder startles with her bloody blade;
Black Carnage sits upon the demon's car,
O'er which the Furies bear his fatal star:
Swift as the wind these monster spirits speed
To glut with blood the roaring mouth of War,
While all their own destructive passions feed,
And revel in the gore, as millions 'round them bleed.

Exulting Fame now builds her throne on high,
And adds the nerve which youthful heroes lack,
And holds in rapturous awe each gazing eye;
But Death, from the hot field awhile held back,
Soon runs his course, and leaves a bloody track;
Before him Glory flees, and Fame withdraws;
The sky, meanwhile, in thick clouds looming black,
And Horror grim fills up the dreadful pause,
As Nature mourns alone her violated laws.

Avaunt the scene: For milder spirits haste
To bid this foul, rebellious combat cease,
And drive Destruction from the gloomy waste.
See mild Affection, with celestial Peace,
While Virtue's smiles bid kindling joys increase;
Stern Justice, rampant o'er the meaner clay,
Balances the follies of man's caprice:—
These, with their countless blessings strew the way,
And heavenly choirs conclude the regenerated day.

LET IT TOLL! LET IT TOLL!

THE church bell tolls: let it toll! let it toll!
For it sounds the dirge of a soldier's soul,
Fleeing to Heaven, as it parteth from clay:
Let the old bell toll, as it fleeth away!

It merrily rang on a bridal morn,
When Happiness flowed from Pleasure's horn;
But now it is sounding the fatal knell,
As the widow has kissed her sad farewell.

Let it toll! let it toll! with its hollow sound,
As the sexton is shaping the newly-made mound:
And a tear for each toll, for a youth lies there—
The mother heart-broken with grief and despair.

Many years ago it swung as slow,
As now it swingeth its notes of woe.
Oh! say, shall it chime and still swing on,
Like a wail for a curse that will never be gone?

Oh! would that its chimes could sound the knell
Of a sin whose woe no tongue can tell:
But the iron that sounds the march of Time
Shall toll o'er the corpse of this national crime.

THE SORROW-STRICKEN VALE.

I see a village by a river's side;
The homely cots strewed o'er the rising knolls;
The white-washed church betokens rustic pride;
The river's glassy face star-mirrored rolls;
From yonder tower the mournful music tolls;
I hear the funeral notes across the water,
Chiming the requiem of gallant souls
Who died in misery, 'mid the day's slaughter,
Without the soothing aid of sister, wife, or daughter.

'Twas a fair sight when through the village street,
With rolling drums, and banners floating gay,
And all the equipage of war complete,
The soldiers marched right gallantly away.
Then the wrinkled matron and the sire gray
Bestowed their blessing on their parting son,
And then at night retired, for him to pray.
Yes! 'twas a glorious sight; but soon 'twas done,
And as the pageant passed, their sorrows had begun.

Ah! there is weeping in that vale to-night,
And bosoms ready with their woes to burst.
Alas! fair maiden, with thine eye once bright,
No more within thy breast may love be nursed;
Of dark despair thy heart now feels the worst:
Thy soldier lover sleeps the sleep of death!
Well may'st thou say of wars, "Be all accurs'd!"
Perchance he called me with his gasping breath?
"I come, my love! I come. But, ha! can this be Death!"

"He died in honor, sir! I saw him fall."
"Ha! you saw him then? Oh! where?" "At the head
Of his brave comrades. At his captain's call
He scaled the heights, and there in honor bled."
"'Twas honor, then? but, ah! you say he's dead!"
Thus, mad with grief, the gray-haired sire spake:
"Keep your honor—give me my boy instead!"
"But, hold! he battled for his country's sake."
My God! must men in blood their savage fury slake?

"Honor? give me my boy! away with fame,
If it is built upon eternal woe.
Give me his life; I'll ask nor noble name,
Nor gaudy wreaths that fickle men bestow!
Makes Fame our happiness on earth? Ah, no!
The glory take, and give his being back!
My own brave boy; and must thy spirit go,
Before its time, along yon devious track?
But that's to Heaven, while I must writhe upon the rack."

Oh! ye who madly pant for martial fame,
With calm reflection for a moment pause,
And think upon the price of such a name.
Say what it is, will be, and what it was;
Trampling on God's, if not on earthly, laws;
And every laurel makes a widow's tear!
It does not matter what may be the cause,
Thy glories still are purchased deadly dear,
And all must rise like ghosts from some poor soldier's bier.

NUPTIAL DIRGE.

WREATHE the roses red and white;
  Pluck the lily from its stem;
For this is Leila's bridal night,
  And fair shall be her diadem!

Bring the robe of purest snow;
  Bind the wreaths with evergreen
Upon her alabaster brow,
  That she may look a bridal queen!

But she slumbers ! yes, her sleep
  Is that which lingers, lasteth long !
The bridegroom comes not here to weep,
  While angels chant her wedding song.

Little thought they, in that hour
  Of parting, plighting still their love,
That sister sprites, with weird power,
  Their woof of fate so darkly wove !

Fell he on Manassas plain,
  Among the few, but gallant dead,
Who braved the victor's iron rain,
  Though no arm their valor led !

Honored be their sacred dust ;
  Shrined in the noblest niche of fame ;
While they who wrecked a people's trust
  Be consigned to lasting shame !

Wreathe the roses red and white;
  Pluck the lily from its stem;
For this is Leila's bridal night,
  And fair shall be her diadem!

THE DYING SOLDIER.

Beneath the roof of tattered tent,
  The wounded soldier lay;
Beside him sat a comrade dear,
  To watch the night away.
The night breeze, on his fevered brow,
  Fell like the breath of Heaven:
As if, to calm his anguished heart,
  An angel's touch was given!

His comrade bathed the painful wound,
  And pressed the thankful hand ;
And watched the soldier's dreamy eyes,
  To catch their least command.
But fainter still the throbbing pulse
  Doth chide the sluggish vein,
And into lethargy doth sink
  The lately racking pain.

He does not reck the loss of limb—
  He does not fear to die ;
But thinking on the absent ones
  Will dim the bravest eye.
And, oh ! the pang when this sad news
  Shall reach her anxious face,
Who built such fond and gallant hopes
  Upon his boyhood's grace !

And close unto his lips are pressed
  Some little treasured thing;
His filmy eyes no more can see
  The raven tress or ring!
The moonlight on the wasted cheek
  A single tear betrays,
That eloquently tells the tale
  Of young Love's sunny days.

His comrade, from his latest breath,
  Receives "Good bye!" for all;
Which he'll convey, unless his fate
  Like him should be to fall!
And angels, then, that fondly wait
  On hearts so brave and true,
In gentle dreams will tell to all
  Each tender, sad adieu!

Oh! thus are beautiful and brave,
Beneath the crash of War,
Like holy martyrs, offered up
To deck the demon's car!
The bravest and the best do fall,
(While cravens turn and flee;)
And, oh! to such the manly heart
Will ever bend the knee!

And shrined in hearts, their gallant deeds
Will grace the path of Time
With incense sweet, that could not rise
From actions more sublime!
And Love, upon their storied urn,
Her tearful tribute pays;
While Glory and immortal Fame
Bestow their greenest bays!

TWILIGHT'S GLOOM.

By the dying embers sitting,
  In that strange, old-fashioned room,
With her fingers slowly knitting,
  In the twilight's deepening gloom,
With her fingers slowly knitting,
  An aged matron sits,
Slowly knitting, slowly knitting,
  As the dusky shadow flits.
As the day to night's embraces
  Slips like the soul away,
That lit with joy the faces
  That could not bid it stay;

As its shadow, slowly flitting,
  Leaves at length the icy clay ;
While, in her chamber sitting.
  Hope lights it on its way.

Oh, her heart is sad with thinking,
  How, in his youthful pride,
Her gallant boy is sinking
  In the battle's rolling tide!
She had a dream but yester-eve,
  As she nodded o'er her knitting,
That made her anxious bosom grieve,
  As she was knitting, slowly knitting.
By the dying embers sitting,
  As she slumbered in her chair,
She dreamed that she was knitting,
Slowly knitting, slowly knitting,
  Wreaths of glory for his hair !

O'er her heart a shadow's flitting,
  That will never lift again;
As her fingers, slowly knitting,
  Catch the falling tears like rain.
Though he fell on field of glory,
  When the conquered column broke,
And his name will grace the story
  Of those gallant hearts of oak!
Yet she knows his face will never
  Cross that homely threshold more;
Though her dreamy eyes forever
  Keep watch upon the door!
As her fingers slowly knitting,
  With her eyes upon the door,
Slowly knitting, slowly knitting,
  Slowly knitting evermore!

MARTIAL DIRGE.

THERE'S music in the martial strain,
When warlike banners fly;
When drum and trumpet clash again,
And nodding plumes go by;
When neighing steeds impatient prance,
And gallant hearts beat high;
As Pity lends a melting glance,
And lovers breathe a sigh.

There's music in the muffled drum,
When flags no longer float;
When all but heart and pulse are dumb,
And language in the throat.
As black as night the sable plume
Plays its melancholy rote;
While o'er the loved one's early tomb,
Muskets peal their parting note!

Home and Camp.

In the dull repose of our changeless life,
I long for passion, I long for strife,
As in the calm the mariner sighs
For rushing waves and groaning skies.
Oh, for the lists, the lists of fame!
Oh, for the herald's glad acclaim;
For floating pennon and prancing steed,
And Beauty's wonder at Manhood's deed.

—Praed.

A SOLDIER'S LIFE FOR ME.

AIR—"*Life on the Ocean Wave.*"

OH! a soldier's life for me,
  Where the thundering cannons roar;
And the banners of the free
  On the fields of battle soar!
At the sound of the kettle drum,
  And the clarion trumpet's peal,
From our peaceful homes we come,
  With our trusty swords of steel.

A life on the tented field,
Where the tramp of the sentinel,
When the distant musket pealed,
Gives note that all is well!
And the soldier's brief repose
Is under a cloudy crown,
Where the struggling moonlight glows,
And the watchful stars look down!

Oh! sad is the soldier's life,
When the din of battle's o'er;
And the brave ones of the strife
Are weltering in their gore:
To think of the loving hearts
Who will wait for their step in vain;
Nor know of the anguished darts
That racked on their bed of pain!

But away with sorrow's tears,
  As the eagles onward sweep!
For the bravest have no fears,
  Though the bravest always weep
At the ghastly heaps of slain,
  And the horrors of the war;
Though o'er the conquered plain
  His own was the victor's star.

Oh! a soldier's life for me,
  And a death on the field of fame,
Ere the cause of our Liberty
  Be bowed by a traitor's shame!
And the flag of the true and brave,
  With its hues of rainbow light,
O'er the land and sea shall wave,
  With its cluster of stars so bright.

ADIEU.

She stood upon the strand,
  Her voice swelled in her throat;
She waved her lily hand,
  As sped the parting boat.

My Edwin, fare thee well!
  Oh! wilt thou faithful be?
Oh! wilt thou think of Nell
  Across the stormy sea?

Fare thee well! my sweetest!
  Nor doubt my constancy;
Still thou'lt be my dearest,
  Till I come back to thee.

If death should be thy fate,
  Where Freedom's banners soar,
My faithful heart shall wait
  In weeds forevermore.

Shed, love, no doubting tear!
  For we shall meet again:
Thy image will be near
  On every battle plain.

THE SOLDIER LOVER'S DREAM.

I DREAMT of thee, my May, last night,
  As slumbering on my straw I lay;
I thought I pledged a bumper bright—
  A cup of wine to rosy May.
Thus ran the pledge I gave to thee,
  As danced the wine within the bowl:
To Beauty's best the toast shall be!
  And with the wine I pledge my soul!

Oh ! shall the glory of my dream,
  When war's loud blasts have ceased to blow,
Above the altar brightly gleam,
  To crown with Hope our nuptial vow?
Whene'er I drink a cup of wine,
  My first, my latest pledge shall be—
While heart and soul are fondly thine—
  My May ! a bumper bright to thee !

OH, ANNIE! WILT THOU WALK WITH ME?

OH, ANNIE! wilt thou walk with me,
  Beside the mossy banks, to-night?
The fresh-mown hay doth smell so sweet,
  The fields are bathed in soft moonlight.
I'll pluck the lily and the rose,
  And twine them in a wreath for thee,
And row thee safe home in my boat,
  If thou'lt but walk this night with me.

I'd ask thee not, my Annie dear,
  To meet me by the river's shore,
But I must bid thee, sweet, good-bye;
  We part, perchance, to meet no more!
My heart is in my country's cause;
  My life will float on battle's tide;
But when returned, with glory crowned,
  Wilt meet me by the river's side?

SONG.

WILL you marry me, Jenny, my darling,
  When the din of the battle is o'er;
And, returned to the hearts that have sorrowed,
  The soldier is happy once more?

Will you marry me, Jenny, my darling,
  If I come back, all shattered, from war;
And hobble along on my crutches,
  And my vision obscured by a scar?

Will you weep for me, Jenny, my darling,
  If my death in the battle you hear;
If I valiantly died with the foremost,
  Will you shed o'er my ashes a tear?

I'll doubt you not, Jenny, my darling!
  I know that you'll ever be true;
And though I come back on my crutches,
  I'll only be dearer to you!

Your tears, that are shining like diamonds,
  Tell plainly those jewels will fall,
If I die, in a shower of sadness,
  And sprinkle, all hallowed, my pall!

IT BREAKS AT LAST.

It breaks at last! It breaks at last!
  The heart oppressed with heavy woe;
Its joys are pictures of the past;
  It sinks beneath this fatal blow!

Like strings of once delicious lyre,
  Where Music all her sweetness shed,—
When careless fingers broke the wire,
  Alas, the throbs of passion fled!

The heart that, to the touch of Love,
  Swelled up with all its wealth divine,
Has ceased with rapture's pulse to move,
  And dies upon its own sad shrine.

Alas! his form on Glory's plain
  Lies in battle's crimson state;
A single one of thousands slain—
  Whose homes are now all desolate!

Oh, could her hand have smoothed his brow!
  Oh, could her smile have lit his face,
Ere angels, hovering to and fro,
  Had robed him in their heavenly grace!

So dear in life, and thus to die,
  With lingering wounds upon the field:—
No one to heed his plaintive cry,
  As thundering cannon o'er him pealed!

It breaks at last, the tender heart,
  And droops unto its martyred mate!—
With Love, that spurned the veil of art,
  She struggled never 'gainst her fate.

Shrine of the Brave.

How sleep the brave, who sink to rest,
By all their country's wishes blest!
When Spring, with dewy fingers cold,
Returns to deck their hallow'd mould,
She there shall dress a sweeter sod
Than Fancy's feet have ever trod.

By fairy hands their knell is rung,
By forms unseen their dirge is sung:
There Honor comes, a pilgrim gray,
To bless the turf that wraps their clay;
And Freedom shall awhile repair,
To dwell a weeping hermit there.

—Collins.

AMBITION.

Ambition proudly claims from all
  Her foll'wers and her humble slaves ;
Nor weeps she when she winds their pall,
  And lays them in forgotten graves.
Her lurid beams more brightly burn
Upon the hero's funeral urn ;
For then the pageant of the dead
Gleams proudly round her guilty head ;
And shadows forth rich, purple light,
That lures souls on to deathlike night.

But in that night, a brilliant star
  Shall shine along the hero's track ;
The brightest glory of the war,
  That looms above its horror black :
The star of Hope, on stormy sea,
Of those that struggle to be free ;
Oh! only then Ambition weaves
Her crowns of amaranthine leaves,
To wreathe the brows of noble youth,
Battling in the cause of Truth.

The pomp of glory, too, shall pass,
  Ere we have marked its splendid noon ;
And sorrow vainly weep, alas !
  O'er garlands faded, all too soon,
Like leaves of Autumn fall, unless
Freedom's flower of loveliness
Shines with its eternal glow
Upon Ambition's open brow ;
Then shall her wreaths grow green with years,
Because refreshed with grateful tears !

THE MAUSOLEUM OF THE BRAVE.

"GLORY be to them that die in this great cause."—CAMPBELL.

FROM the long line of bright historic names,
That down upon us, from their splendid past—
Whose all of glory's now immortal fame's—
Loom up like mountains in their grandeur vast,
The noblest of them all is he who stood,
Deaf to all but honor's stern command,
Like a firm rock against Rebellion's flood,
That threatened to o'erwhelm his native land!

They have become the prophets of all time!
Unto the curtained ages have they spoken
Of the immortal pathway t' the sublime,
Ere their mysterious shell is broken.
But, when revealed, how gloriously there
Their mighty shades! The same through countless years;
And the laurel wreath still as green and fair,
As when first watered by a nation's tears.

When History's golden tablet, ages hence,
The grandeur of your martyred lives displays,
She will exhaust her art's omnipotence,
To speak of your deeds in deserving praise.
Oh! could more splendid mausoleum be—
More enduring than monumental brass:
Freedom's martyrs to live in memory,
As if reflected in eternal glass!

Not that you came, as soldiers always come ;
  Not that you fell, as soldiers always fall ;
When trumpet answered to the kettle-drum,
  And the front of battle gleamed a fiery wall :
But rushing to defend a noble cause,
  Against the brother of your hand and heart ;
For faith so true, what meed of poor applause
  Could fitting balm to wound so deep impart ?

Naught but the record of immortal Truth,
  Who shall enshrine you on her holy page ;
When in the promise of your love and youth,
  Your blood your country's troubles did assuage ;
Could justice do to your heroic life!
  And she will weep, that language fails to tell
Of the stern virtues of this bitter strife ;
  Of martyred saints whom Freedom loved so well !

Though you may fall amid the crash of war,
  A single one of many thousands slain,
Your dust will be kissed by the same sweet star,
  That fondly shines upon your native plain!
Where trusting hearts, upon the midnight air,
  For those on tented field they love so well,
Have breathed a maiden's, sire's, and matron's
    prayer;
  While the star on all shines the sad farewell.

Though but a trifling atom you may seem,
  To note amid the dreadful carnage vast,
Our finite reason may not lightly deem
  The purpose of your death was vainly cast.
To Him who noteth e'en the sparrow's fall,
  There is no act of life without intent:—
We cannot know the part designed for all,
  Who may be in this crimson burial blent.

The glory that shall stoop unto your brows ;
  The tears, that grateful millions, yet unborn,
Shall blend in homage with their earnest vows,
  To keep the heritage you transmit unshorn,
The world has never seen. For never was,
  Since hoary Time his circling course began,
For man a war to wage, more hallowed cause—
  The fight of Freedom for the Rights of Man !

LOVE'S PILGRIMAGE. (4)

THOUGH green's the turf above their lonely graves;
  Though sadly sighs the night-wind through the
    trees;
And moans the river with its rippling waves,
  Unto the music of the sobbing breeze;

Though on their field of glory, in their pride,
  When the wild sea of carnage floated by,
By Death's keen sickle garnered side by side,
  Upon the breast of Mother Earth they lie;

Though memory keeps their story ever green,
And all heroic makes each humble life,
That bore its part, throughout the swelling scene,
Of that unequal and disastrous strife ;

Though Love comes hither, on her angel wings,
With grateful tears their trampled graves to bless;
And o'er their dust a mournful requiem sings ;
Weeping away her soul's rich tenderness :

The good and brave should sleep their final sleep
Beneath the shadow of their stricken home ;
That those who miss them from the hearth may weep
Above their ashes in all time to come.

That woman's tender hand the flowers may trail
In clinging festoons o'er the honored dust ;
And as she, weeping, tells the mournful tale,
Commit his glory to his children's trust !

Their mangled forms the barbarians spurn,
And dead and dying, from the gory plain,
Are headlong hurled into a common urn—
Nothing to mark the promiscuous slain!

Alas! that there should bear the name of man,
The wretch who little cares how bosoms bleed!
Is all that chivalry upon the wan,
That could not brook a mercenary deed?

Their ashes mingled with the earth, alone
Their names are left for us to cherish here;
We cannot mark their graves with sculptured stone;
We cannot rest their clay on Honor's bier.

Oh! like a shadow did these heroes pass!
Yet left on Memory's glass a fadeless trace;
Where Love may turn, as Sorrow cries, alas!
And view their youthful manhood's matchless grace.

And Love shall wend her holy pilgrimage,
When summer in her flowery robe appears,
Like faithful palmer in the knightly age,
Unto that battle-field through coming years.

And though their resting-place she knoweth not,
The whole vast plain her woe will consecrate;
Because their sacred bones all scattered rot,
And earth receives as seed their ashes great;

Whose soil henceforth shall only be—thus blest—
The freeman's unconquerable abode;
Where millions yet unborn shall safely rest,
And worship then their Freedom and their God.

How sadly, in beseeching violet,
Love sees reflected the last, fond adieu,
They looked unto the skies, ere coldly set
Their longing, dreamy eyes, in deathly hue!

Oh, do not lightly deem Love's labor vain !
For what were this cold world without her tears ?
When sinks the soul beneath its mortal pain,
Love's smiles dispel the cloud of doubts and fears.

Oh, Love has been the cherished amulet
Of lord and vassal, since the world began ;
The weird charm above his fortunes set—
For weal or woe, the angel of the man !

Back to the soldier's home, now desolate—
Her faithful memory stored with these sad scenes—
She comes like galleon with her precious freight,
And o'er the anguished heart in pity leans.

When mortal grief becomes thus sanctified,
It is as if some holy dream were true ;
When, in the beauty of their manly pride,
We see them float in clouds of Glory's hue.

And Love will faithful tend her vestal lamp,
  And keep their garlands green with constant tears,
While o'er their ashes, with historic tramp,
  Looms up the grandeur of the cycling years!

Shadows of Destiny.

If ye do not hope, ye will not find: for in despairing, ye block up the mine at its mouth, ye extinguish the torch, even when ye are already in the shaft.

GOD and the world we worship still together,
  Draw not our laws to Him, but His to ours;
Untrue to both, so prosperous in neither,
  The imperfect will brings forth but barren flowers!
Unwise as all distracted interests be,
Strangers to God, fools in humanity:
Too good for great things, and too great for good,
While still "*I dare not*" waits upon "*I would.*"

—COLERIDGE.

OH! LIGHTLY LIES THE HEAD AT NIGHT.

Oh! lightly lies the head at night,
  That doth a goodly deed that day;
And calmly beats the heart that's right,
  And ne'er from Virtue's folds doth stray.

Oh! never yet has God-like Truth
  Unfaithful been to those who own,
To honored age from early youth,
  Her power, and worship at her throne.

Dishonor wins a brief success,
  And vainly struts in stolen plume;
But soon its glittering glâre grows less—
  Then fades into forgotten tomb.

Go forth, brave youth! thy banner be
  As fair as stainless knight ere bore,
In vaunted lists of chivalry,
  In the gallant days of yore!

For Fame will never bind her wreath
  On brows that have ignoble been;
They pass to unregretted death,
  And leave behind no laurel green.

Oh! ye who fight life's battles here,
  Be ever true to Honor's call;
And when you rest upon your bier,
  A people's mourners bear your pall.

HOPE'S GUERDON.

To THE battle rushed they forth,
Sturdy legions of the North,
From their fields of golden grain, and their mountains capped with snow!
As the torrent fiercely flowed,
Looked they as they onward rode,
Where the drums were wildly beating, with their bosoms all aglow.

As the sullen thunder breaks,
Ere the rumbling mountain quakes ;
When the fiery pitch is seething, and is boiling underneath,
The gathering cry arose,
When they rushed upon their foes,
Like the flow of red-hot lava—the harbinger of death !

Who can breast the torrent's tide,
Freedom's hosts may turn aside
From the channel, that is deepened by the flow of many tears.
In her splendor and her might,
Like an angel in the night,
To all that watch and pray for her, she faithfully appears.

When the Summer's come and gone,
And the Autumn weeps alone,
Her brows with plenty crowned, for the beauty's faded pride;
So, when Freedom's battle's o'er,
Though her flags in triumph soar,
Her heart is anguished at the wreck of battle's crimson tide.

When the promised buds of youth
Unfold the flower of Truth,
And the beacon lamps of Freedom, burning brightly, never wan,
Oh! her flag will be unfurled,
In its glory, o'er the world,
And from Oppression's ashes rise the equal rights of man!

Yes! Freedom's waves will ever
Flow onward like a river!
Who'd be immortal must upon its heaving bosom float.
But if, in the shifting sands,
They dream on with idle hands,
Of their inglorious slothfulness the future hath no note.

When the night was cold and dark,
Did your watchful eyes ne'er mark
The clouds that floated o'er the sky reveal a brilliant star?
So, for woes of bitter years,
Through the murky cloud appears
The star of Hope, as recompense for carnage of the war!

HALTING IN THE BREACH.

Halting in the breach
 In the traitors' wall;
Will no lesson teach,
 But your country's fall?

Wait you for the night
 That shall surely come,
Ere you, for the Right,
 Strike the demon dumb?

Only backward turn,
  Hearts of craven hue,
That could never learn
  Promptings good and true!

Souls of God-like stamp,
  Guide with steady speed,
Like a faithful lamp,
  In their country's need.

Halt you never, then;
  Rend the cloud in two;
And, like honest men,
  Fight the battle through!

THE SHADOW OF NEMESIS.

LIKE snow-flakes from the eternal clouds,
That wrap the earth in fleecy shrouds,
God's blessings fall alike on man,
Throughout his mortal measure's span;
And when the battle here is o'er,
And lord and slave are known no more,
The pure in heart share equal love,
In the blue vault that shines above!

And who shall say that this green earth,
When life and nature teemed her birth,
With ample room for all mankind,
The spoil of tyrants was designed?
Finite eyes may not perceive
The threads that fates mysterious weave;
But, rest assured, the hand of time
Will all unfold their web sublime.

Nemesis, struggling in the cloud,
That seemeth like our country's shroud,
May rend the gloom, like lightning's glare,
While serpent splendors of her hair
Doth run throughout the stricken land,
The heralds of her vengeful hand,
That rights the wrong, and dries the tears
That flowed through long and bitter years!

When He has garnered up His sheaves,
Nothing of His harvest leaves:
The poor beside the rich shall stand;
Within the slave's, the master's hand!
Then do not doubt, that still shall shine
The splendor of this light divine
Upon the custom-clouded brain,
And break at once each bondman's chain!

THE FALL OF FEUDALISM.

How DEEP the throbs which thrill the wand'rer's
vein,
Who, melancholy, roves a distant strand,
And hears, in some half-sung, half-chanted strain,
The well-known music of his native land!
A spell, as if by an enchanter's wand,
Enwraps the soul; while passes to the view
Life's younger days, on which the chilling hand
Of Time has left no blast. Their early hue
Looks yet as green and bright as Fancy ever drew.

There is a spell in Music's gentle tone,
Which calls the phantoms up of what has been;
But sweetest far when listening alone,
And sadly sweet when absent from the scene.
Who has not felt, as Summer's air serene,
Some plaintive strain, across still waters bore,
His nerves beat high, with quickened tremor keen?
'Twas such sensations thrilled the bosom's core
Of Lestocq, as he paced, strange, on a stranger's shore.

It was an air some simple rustic sang;
But he had heard it on the banks of Rhine,
When the cup was quaffed, and the loud laugh rang,
'Mong the dancers 'neath the autumnal vine.
But where are they, while he is left to pine
Alone, and friendless, from his land exiled,
The last descendant of a humble line?
Perished in Freedom's cause; their homes defiled,
And kingly castles high above their corpses piled!

What owns man here beyond a breath of air ?
Was this fair earth designed for tyrant kings,
Who seize a kingdom for their princely share,
Their only joy to point Oppression's stings,
Nor heed the woes their rank injustice brings
Upon their fellow-men ; nor fear possess
For God nor man, so that the glitt'ring wings
Of Glory seem their damning cause to bless,
While Fame, reluctant, yields her magic seal's impress ?

Base scourgers of the world ! when man shall wake
From dark Submission's sleep ; when he shall see
And feel himself oppressed ; when he shall shake
The shackles from his mind, and stand forth free,
Untrammeled, in his native dignity,
Claiming an equal right with all the world,
Then, ye foul oppressors ! then shall there be
A gladsome shout, while Freedom's flag's unfurl'd,
And kings and sceptres all from thrones polluted hurled !

I saw a rocky height beleaguered 'round
By Freedom's friends; their number, few at first,
Increased by scores, until the swelling sound
Of countless men with resolution burst
Like ocean's roar. To know and bear the worst
Of human ills had been their hapless lot;
But tyrants, chains, and slavery had nursed
Aspiring hopes above their servile cot;
And dreams of liberty can never be forgot.

Black was the feudal fortress on the steep—
The sun almost refused on it to shine:—
How many chained within that prison weep,
While lords and ladies wassail with their wine!
A little luxury they might resign
To clothe the naked and the hungry feed.
Away! 'twould be a humbling of their line;
They are the peers; a peasant but a weed,
For them to sweat and toil, for them to groan and bleed!

Above the gloomy walls, with sullen wave,
A gorgeous banner dallied on the air;
But it shall be a shroud—those stones a grave—
For all that lightly laugh and revel there ;
And nothing left to tell the future where
They mould'ring lie. 'Tis willed, and it shall
be ;
For Retribution's arm doth never spare ;
Its deeds are reckoned in eternity ;
Too deep its workings are for poor humanity.

Hark to the clam'rous shouts ! the din of arms !
See the proud banners glitt'ring in the sun,
While the roused soldiers' fierce and loud alarms
Tell plainly that the conflict's now begun !
Who shall first proclaim that parapet won ?
With panting hopes a thousand hearts beat high ;
But e'en among that gallant crowd is one
Who perils all upon a single die ;
Freely he dares the worst, and yet he knows not
why.

But I could tell, while pointing to the days
Of that brave patriot's youth; I could unfold
Unto his startled and astonished gaze
A strange picture: The prison bell has tolled;
A moment—the axe falls—and dumb and cold
Lies one who battled for his country's sake.
The winding sheet none but the widow rolled;
For Slav'ry freezes up men's hearts. Awake!
Thou art his son; arise, to arms, and vengeance take!

A guardian spirit brooding o'er the scene
I saw upon a mountain near the sky;
Around her head the lightning flashes keen,
And at her feet the thunder rumbles by!
Unmoved by aught, she looks, with steadfast eye,
Upon the living mass of men below;
She cheers the brave with smiles; when one would fly,
Night's blackness sits upon her frowning brow.
That patriot's deeds have flushed her cheek with crimsoned glow.

She stops to see his young ambition dare
The perilous leap, and leave his mates behind;
Then sweeps the cloud-girt height, so wildly fair,
Her tresses floating on the wanton wind,
Her robe flies loose—no clasping girdles bind;
Hygean smiles glow on her rosy cheek,
The piercing eye proclaims the free-born mind;
And her clear, mellow voice, nor harsh, nor weak,
Sounds like a spirit strain above the mountain's peak.

Immeasurably great, Spirit of the Free!
Pervading each and everything of earth,
Thy glorious essence in yon form I see,
The emblem of thy beauty and thy worth,
Who sweep'st unchained the realms that gave
her birth,
The medium betwixt the world and heaven,
Unpoisoned air! propitious type! though dearth
May mark the march of kings, and links be driven
To bind mankind, by thee those chains shall yet be
riven.

The serpent lightning leaps from rock to rock,
In brilliant flashes 'round that spirit's head,
While far below those bands, in dreadful shock
Oppose the front of war, and with the dead
Many a soldier finds a wakeless bed;
At every gasp of death that spirit weeps,
And more for brows her hand has garlanded.
Freedom cannot move, like yon lightning leaps;
The growth is slow, but sure the harvest that she reaps.

So long, it seemed as if whole ages there
Those hosts embattled for the breath of life;
And all the while that form in nether air
Cheered her flagging bands to renew the strife,
Nor fear the horrors of the opposing knife;
For all must struggle, who would dare be free,
And the cause is, though just, with danger rife.
A thunderbolt dispelled my phantasy;
I woke to find, on earth, still chains and slavery.

Willing to bear the yoke of laws that be,
If but tempered with Wisdom's kindly hand,
They hope for better days, yet bend the knee
Unto the feudal lord of all the land,
Yielding obedience to each demand;
But, like that basil that is sweet to smell
Untouched, yet bitter if 'tis crushed, they stand
Ready to serve their lord, and serve him well;
Still, if a tyrant proves, each voice shall sound his knell.

Whatever clime may boast itself as free,
Whatever soul can love the noble deed;
Whenever minstrels breathe their Poesy,
Wherever slaves are praying to be freed,
Wherever Freedom casts her fruitful seed,
On land or barques that brave the stormy sea,
Man's, woman's heart, will o'er your mis'ries bleed,
And oft through coming years the pledge shall be,
In cot or festive hall, the Defenders of the Free!

Lyrics for Freedom.

PURPOSE so barr'd, it follows,
Nothing is done to purpose : therefore, beseech you,
You that will be less fearful than discreet,
That love the fundamental part of state,
More than you doubt the change on't, that prefer
A noble life before a long, and wish
To jump a body with a dangerous physic
That's sure of death without it, at once pluck out
The multitudinous tongue : let them not lick
The sweet which is their poison. Your dishonor
Mangles true judgment, and bereaves the state
Of that integrity which should become it,
Not having the power to do the good it would,
For th' ill which doth control it.

—CORIOLANUS.

THE SONG OF LABOR.

YES! though gold be master now,
  Labor yet shall have its own:
Patient toil shall strike the blow,
  That levels down the tyrant's throne.

Freedom's not for one, but all!
  The earth was given by God to man;
And, though some may be in thrall,
  Oppression's night is on the wan.

Courage! then; be steadfast, true,
  Ye who delve, who dig, and spin,
A brighter day shall dawn for you;
  Your rights on earth ye yet shall win.

Hope not soon to gain the prize:
  Justice comes, though slow, but sure.
On the future fix your eyes:
  Night cannot for aye endure.

Flesh may waste, and death may come;
  Falter not, for these shall be
The last of woes, that form the sum,
  That breaks your chains, and makes you free!

Courage! then, nor fear the end:
  In patience wait, in patience pray;
God has ever been your friend,
  And He'll unroll your justice day.

THE PATRIOT'S PRAYER.

Columbia, weep, that Slavery's hated crime
In deepest dye of foul, unnatural stain
Should be emblazoned on thy book of time!
Freer the world has grown, and Slavery's chain
No more bids murder stalk across the main,
Where gauntest misery in frenzy glowed,
Closing the fest'ring links of mortal pain.
No more doth shrinking Commerce bear the load
Of human flesh and blood on swift destruction's road.

E'en when the vaunted empress of the sea,
Whose countless sails remotest ocean sweep,
Has washed from her shrine the foul iniquity,
Must she still sleep, the noblest country sleep,
While Freedom's guardian angels blushing weep?
Lives none to pluck the venom at its source?
Men we have who'd dare the Tarpeian leap,
But few to feel a shadow of remorse:
And doth Columbia own no giant WILBERFORCE?

Can custom always reign? Believe it not.
There is a better time for earth; man may
Fetter his fellow, but 'tis ne'er forgot;
And Retrospection's view brings on the day
When merit only makes superior clay.
To see the unworthy past, will man incite
To tear the flimsy gauze of sin away—
Acknowledging no thought but what is right;
And then indeed the earth looms up from Error's
night.

Stern Justice banishes each paltry fear,
Obedient to the calls of her high trust;
While Mercy reasons with her softest tear.
Pause, Columbia; ask if it is just
That one should toil to please another's lust.
Dost say 'tis true? Then where does Justice dwell,
If she thus leaves to shame man's meaner dust?
Or has she aped some common fiend of hell,
And to her former self has sighed a last farewell?

But "we are free;" so would our poets sing;
And thundered such by each aspiring sage—
Free as the soarings of our eagle's wing;
Free as the lion in his iron cage;
Nay, as the puppet on his wired stage.
Just were our sires; an expedient rule,
Blessed by the tutorings of a backward age,
Has taught us justice in another school;
Of each ambitious knave we're made the pliant tool!

Oh! may not penitential years erase
The spots that soil our fame?—for soiled it is;
When slav'ry dare not show its Gorgon face;
But order startles. Anarchy is this,
When man enjoys his manumission's bliss?
Old th' institution is. Unhappy time,
When man will not his craven fears dismiss;
But still must cringe and tolerate a crime,
And let his manhood sink in sycophantic slime.

Oh! how it makes me blush for man, to see
Some whining sniv'ler pand'ring body, soul,
And all that makes him God's image, that he
May bask in public favor: while the whole
Inertia of his acts tends to control
And bury conscience! Is he a man, whose noon,
Whose prime of life, nor heeds that inward toll,
That strikes the noble mind, but who will soon
Kneel at the foot of power, and crave a beggar's
boon?

Then let me be a dog, and lick the hand
That feeds me; for of all I do detest
The sycophant, that serpent of the land:
To be a dog, is to be among the best
Of brutes; but he's of mankind the meanest:
A paltry villain and a truckling knave.
And doth Columbia cherish at her breast
Such scorpions; and doth her banner wave
Alike o'er shameless deeds and o'er the Patriot's
Grave?

Thou shalt not lie; but Truth's Damascean blade
Should not be wielded in too bold a sun,
Lest too much light may make mankind afraid.
'Tis not by force the battle's always won;
Yet he who loves the world will never shun,
Of scanning well the passing time, the task;
To cure distemper ere the root's begun;
Nor shrink to tear aside the slavish mask
That screens from public scorn this fatal basilisk!

Peace to the Past: the Future be thy hope.
'Tis ne'er too late from error to recede.
Too deeply hast thou revelled. The fell scope
Of passion unrestrained, has made thee bleed
What ages cannot cleanse. Thy present need
A giant mind, of the old Roman hue.
Not one who swayeth like the toppling reed;
But, like th'unbending oak, be constant, true,
And capable to see with clear, expansive view.

What, if thy children's tears in rivers run,
Will fading hope now sink, nor rise again
To be the herald of thy future sun?
His bones may whiten earth; but not in vain
The death of him in Freedom's battles slain.
His wasted ashes lie on Honor's bier,
'Neath the proud canopy of Glory's fane:
Unnumbered hearts the patriot's deeds revere,
And to his memory drop Affection's welcome tear!

His name's a legacy, that Hist'ry's page
(Not with the weight of fulsome praises bowed)
Bequeaths, exulting, to a future age!
His grave's the world—eternity his shroud;
Blessed by the lowly, worshipped by the proud;
The bane of kings—whose monument's their shame;
His station fixed above the common crowd;
No tongue can taint—no scathing years defame—
The amaranthine wreaths that cluster round his name!

THE TAX-PAYER'S SONG. (5)

AFTER HOOD'S "SONG OF THE SHIRT."

TAX, tax, tax,
While foul contractors steal:
Tax, tax, tax,
Though the poor may want a meal!
Oh, little they care for the woe
This horrible war on all
Doth cast with its leaden blow
A suffocating pall.

Tax, tax, tax,
All that administers to life
Tax, tax, tax,
Many years after this strife.
And when the hair is turning gray,
The only legacy we can bequeath,
To the starving children we all shall leave,—
Arrears of our taxes to pay!

Oh, what are we fighting for, in sooth?
To rivet the bondman's chains
The closer by all the blood that's spilt,
While traitorous sword, with its bloody
hilt,
Gleams like Fate, in its speckled stains,
And slaughters our noblest youth?
And the clink in the taxman's cup
Keeps time with the clanking chain;
While all the glory we've garnered up
Are our heaps of ghastly slain!

Oh God! that a Christian's hand,
  Because flesh is of different hue,
Should endanger a peaceful land,
  To fetter his fellow anew!
But, oh! it's more horribly base
  To neglect the nation's weal;
And, like a miserable, craven race,
  At the idol of Slavery kneel!
Was it ever a thousand years,
  That a people beneath the yoke,
Saw no sunlight above their tears,
  That their frozen bondage broke?

    Tax, tax, tax,
  Whatever we eat or drink:
    Tax, tax, tax,
  Till our weary bodies sink.
Oh! better our skins were black,
  And be free from this abject sin,
Than to turn like cowards back,
  From the triumph our cause might win!

Taxed in his swaddling clothes ;
  Taxed in his winding sheet ;
So the horrible system grows ;
  But is never, oh ! never complete !
Yes ! the villainous, vampire crew,
  If they could, would make the air
We breathe, and the sunlight too,
  Their portion of taxes bear !

    Tax, tax, tax,
  Till we're nothing but skin and bone ;
    Tax, tax, tax,
  Till the heart has turned to stone.
While the hungry vultures strip
  The national carcass clean,
And with lying heart, but plausible lip,
  They stoop to anything mean ;
Or, like pirates would scuttle the ship,
  If the deed would not be seen,
That their pockets might clink with the
    yellow gold,
The price of their betters in bondage sold !

It's oh! what a sickening sight!
  Our blood like water poured,
While a reckless, rusting blight
  Eateth the nation's sword!
Oh, would that the words of song
  Were keen as the lightning's darts,
To wither the ruthless wrong,
  And shatter the traitorous hearts!

The widow with shilling a day,
  And the orphan in poverty's rags,
Their portion of taxes must pay,
  As the weary life onward drags!
Though the husband and father in war,
  Like martyr, had laid down his life;
And smiled to think that his sinking star
  Showed the way to the end of the strife.
But little he thought, as he lay,
  On his death-bed of fame so gory,
That his children at some future day
  Would be taxed to pay for his glory:

While the villainous rebel crew,
  Whose power he helped to break,
Would coil 'round the nation anew,
  Like a foul and loathsome snake!

Lives there the man who would not share
  The last of his bread and purse,
To have his country's honor fair,
  And free from this blighting curse?
Let the taxman come! We'll freely give,
  And toil till we're skin and bone,
If you'll only let the nation live
  In Liberty's path alone;
And bid the clanking chains begone,
As the nation in glory marches on!

TWO OR THREE MILLIONS OF DOLLARS A DAY! (6)

Two or three millions of dollars a day!
And a year almost has floated away,
And on the brink the nation stands,
Stilling the waves with waving hands!
            While the breakers roar,
            And dash on the shore!
The laurels we might have won faded away;
Freedom's hopes all turned to ashes gray;

When, spite of treasure and of blood,
  In this atrocious conflict lost,
The nation stands where first it stood,
  Its house by the same curse still crossed!

Two or three millions of dollars a day!
Enough to have washed the sin away,
Which still, like a nightmare on the brain,
Will press on the people its clanking chain!
    Your children and mine
    For years will pine,
Like the wandering children of Israel,
Till the Lord shall sound their bondage knell,
  Beneath the doubly painful weight,
    The sin all black upon the brow,
  And paying for—oh! cruel fate!—
    The recklessness that seals it now!

Two or three millions of dollars a day!
And what are we fighting for, I pray?
Two or three millions of dollars a day!
That's what we're fighting for, they say!
Because it won't do,
Say the snivelling crew,
To interfere with this holy trust,
Though our banner it dragged in the dust,
And at the nation's throat, with knife,
Like a blustering footpad stood,
Threatening to take that nation's life,
Unless it dealt in flesh and blood!

KNOCKING THEM DOWN.(7)

Knocking them down!
Knocking them down!
With as steady a knock,
As the stroke of a clock,
From the slaver's block,
Knocking them down!
A family of four,
With their eyelids sore
With the tears, whose track
You could trace on the black

Skin, that would burst
With the woe, if it durst;
But the slaver stands
With a whip in his hands,
So they only moan,
With a wail as keen as a dart,
That would move a stone;
But never a slaver's heart!

Knocking them down!
Knocking them down!
With as steady a knock,
As the stroke of a clock,
From the slaver's block,
Knocking them down!
Weeping so piteously,
With her child on her knee;
To and fro rocking,
With a grief so shocking,
That the eye that could bear,
The heart breaking there,

With an unmoved stare,
Must from demon glare!
But the trader heeds not,
As he picks o'er the lot
Of women and men,
In the slaver's pen,
The plaintive appeals
From that rag-covered woe,
Who asks, while she kneels,
If her daughter *must* go?
What recks he the pain,
As he counteth his gain;
As he feasteth his eyes
On the maiden prize;
And smiles in scorn,
As their hearts are torn?
And the cloud of their sorrow
That's o'er them to-day,
Will enfold them to-morrow,
When they're scattered away!

Knocking them down!
Knocking them down!
With as steady a knock,
As the stroke of a clock,
From the slaver's block,
Knocking them down!
Men, children and all,
From the block must fall;
If willing or not,
'Tis the blackman's lot,
To be bought and sold,
For the trader's gold!
Like a fattened beast,
For epicure's feast,
Man's flesh and blood
On the block is stood;
That dealers in hearts
May see whom to buy;
While the chartered lie
Maketh their shamble carts

A holy, but costly trust,
That eateth away, like rust,
The nation. But woe betide
The wretch who'd dare deride
So goodly a thing, d'ye see,
For a land of Liberty!

Knocking them down!
Knocking them down!
With as steady a knock,
As the stroke of a clock,
From the slaver's block,
Knocking them down!
But the time has come,
At the tap of the drum,
For drying the tears
That have flowed for years;
And cleansing the stain,
That the godless gain

Has left on the soul
Far worse than a ghoul
That feasts on the dead;
For this vampire's fed
On the life-blood warm,
And the maiden charm,
That are chained within
The bars of this sin!

But the time has come for knocking it down,
From the foot of the idol to top of its crown!
And we'll laugh to see, when the Juggernaut falls,
How 'twill crush each miserable worm that crawls,
Spewing his venom against the Right,
Hoping no day will follow the night;
But stumbling his way, 'neath the sinful load
On his spotted heart, like the speckled toad!
But a suffering people will joy to see,
The work going on so dexterously—

Knocking them down!
Knocking them down!
With as steady a knock,
As the stroke of a clock,
From the slaver's block,
Knocking them down!

Among the Lowly.

Alas! I have walked through life
  Too heedless where I trod;
Nay, helping to trample my fellow-worm,
  And fill the burial sod—
Forgetting that even the sparrow falls
  Not unmarked of God!

Each pleading look, that long ago
  I scanned, with a heedless eye,
Each face was gazing as plainly there
  As when I passed it by:
Woe, woe for me, if the past should be
  Thus present, when I die!

—Hood's "Lady's Dream."

THE CABIN DOOR.

WILL we never see our sister, will we never see
her more;
When we gather in the evening, around the cabin
door;
To eat the corn, and sing the song, when daily
work is done?
For, oh! we have such happy times at setting of
the sun!

We thought it strange, when master came to take
her yesterday,
That she should cry so bitterly, and beg to let her
stay;
She surely would come back again, she said she
loved us so;
'Twould break her heart, she knew it would, if she
was forced to go!

Have they sold her, mother? oh! have they sold
our sister Bess?
And will they take no pity on your own and our
distress?
Won't they let her come sometimes, just to join us
in our play?
And then, you know, when she goes home, we'll
run with her half way!

I fear, alas! my little ones, you'll never see her
more,
Unless, like her, you're sold to go to Mississippi's
shore;
And you may chance to see her then, if she should
live so long,
But grief, I think, will kill her soon, for she was
never strong!

Oh! had she been, like you, my child, a shade or
two more dark,
The prowling hound would not have set on her
his fatal mark!
And offer gold on gold to lure my master from his
word;
And take my darling child away, like closely pri-
soned bird!

Oh! never more will these old eyes behold her
smiling face;
But I'll carry to the grave with me the memory
of its grace!
And we'll pray to meet in heaven, though on the
earth no more,
As we gather in the evening, around the cabin
door!

Oh God! will there no morning come to night so
dark and long?
And shall the weak forever be the victim of the
strong?
Oh! will not vengeance fall on men, whose flesh
and blood is sold,
That they may lead a lustful life in purple, wine,
and gold?

UNDER THE PINE-TREE'S SHADE.

ALL under the pine-tree's shade,
  When the fire-flies flash at eve,
And the moonbeams on the glade
  Their shadowy silver leave,

We've danced till the moon went down,
  With our maids of dusky hue;
On their brows the leafy crown,
  On their breasts the love-knot true.

We've little to call our own,
  Not even our hearts or hands;
Which had better be pulseless stone,
  Than be crushed by Slavery's bands!

The love 'neath the pine-tree's shade,
  No matter how fond it be,
In silence had better have laid,
  Than be shattered so ruthlessly.

All under the pine-tree's shade,
  In anguish I bend the knee,
And pray that my sorrowful maid,
  In Heaven may come back to me!

To England, These:

Still one great clime, in full and free defiance,
Yet rears her crest, unconquer'd and sublime,
Above the far Atlantic. She has taught
Her Esau-brethren that the haughty flag,
The floating fence of Albion's feebler crag,
May strike to those whose red right hands have bought
Rights cheaply earned with blood.

—Byron.

A HOMELY EPISTLE FROM BROTHER JONATHAN TO JOHN BULL.

Oh, Johnny Bull! my cotton friend, what is the matter now—
The thickening war-clouds gathering upon your burly brow?
Oh, are you like your Irish boys, whene'er they see a fight,
Just tumble in, because they want to keep the shindy right?
Or have you got some ancient grudge, and wish to have it out,
And through your double face have helped to bring this war about?
Or is your aristocracy afraid the rights of man
Will put your titled privilege beneath their iron ban?

And, therefore, when you thought that we had
quite enough to do,
You'd just step in, and show us how you'd put us
Yankees through!
And laugh to see your rival clipped upon the land
and main—
Your tyrant flag be dominant o'er all the sea again!

But, Johnny, did it e'er occur, my sometime friend,
to you,
Your French ally might chance to know a cunning
trick or two?
That he, to get you in a fix, might very friendly
seem,
That he all latitude might have for his ambitious
scheme?
Besides, I think that Waterloo will be avenged
some day,
And English blood, and honor, too, a terrible reck-
oning pay!

So, Johnny Bull, my cotton friend, I simply say, beware ;
The lion cannot look too sharp for cunning fox's snare !
You say you are the champion of everything that's free ;
Though, I confess, the truth of that I ne'er could clearly see.
Of that black conclave you were one, to chop brave Poland up ;
And helped to make poor shattered France drain down the Bourbon cup !
And Holland, too, who once had swept your Channel with a broom,
You stooped to carve a paltry throne from her dismembered doom.
Of course that was in full accord with your high-sounding fame ;
To me it looked like poor revenge—a nation's meanest shame !

Your Indian empire, John, has been for scandal far and wide,
Of all your thorns the deepest one that rankles in your side.
The slavery on my own old farm is surely bad enough;
Your Indian system is made up of far more damning stuff!
Our slaves are not subjected to a life-blood drying tax,
Collected by the aid of foul inquisitorial racks!
I only quote your writers John, for such atrocities;
To read the cool narration makes the very life-blood freeze!

I know it is not very kind to air your dirty clothes,
And thrust all your nuisances before the public nose;
But when you act so saint-like, John, the world should surely know,
That as a consummate hypocrite you're not so very slow!

Your opium trade was Christian-like, when, on
their bended knees,
You crammed the drug into the throats of misera-
ble Chinese!
Why don't you follow out the plan laid down by
WILBERFORCE?
It certainly would be of all the most illustrious
course.
But, mince it as you may, John Bull, your honor's
pocket deep,
And he who clinks the yellow gold will put your
soul to sleep.
It is not that your people starve—they always have
and will,
As long as aristocracy must have its cormorant
fill!
And flesh and blood be valued at about two-pence
a day,
Scarce giving food enough to keep grim, wolfish
Want at bay!

Your flag was not insulted, John ; a grievance you
have none ;
For we but did precisely, oh! as you have always
done!
Disguise it as you will, your course from meaner
motives spring ;
Although your lordly ones would scorn to stoop to
such a thing.
'Tis patent to the dullest brain, you're jealous of
our power,
And thought on some pretext you'd seize the van-
tage of the hour,
To serve at once your selfish ends, and deal the
deadly blow,
That fills your gaping pockets, John, and lays our
empire low :—
And to this end your arms would take the harlot
Slavery,
And set your iron hoofs upon the struggles of the
free!

Oh, has that vaunted English pride so groveled in
the dust,
And has the sword of ancient days sunk in dishonored rust?
No CROMWELL now doth hold the reins, nor yet a
high-toned PITT;
But creatures of your Cotton lords upon your
benches sit.
We know your aristocracy, if they could have
their way,
Would plunge your people recklessly, headlong
into the fray;
But held in check by those whom their assumption
would despise,
Their course necessitated, is by some mistaken wise.

The poorest worm, 'tis said, will at some bitter
insult turn;
And think you that the smouldering flames will not
break out and burn,

That fired your English yeomanry upon so many fields,
When they bore the glory of your name upon their gallant shields;—
As they think how widens still the breach between the high and low,
And strike the wrongs of many years in one all-crushing blow ?
Although this is prospective, John, I think the world will say,
That, like all other noisy dogs, you've surely had your day!

That campaign in the Crimea, John, was very bad for you;
It showed the world how little of the art of war you knew.
The Frenchmen won the laurels, while your burly English pride
Scarce 'scaped disgrace when onward rolled the battle's surging tide.

In your contracted island, John, you've been so
long content,
We cant' expect your mind at once to grasp a
continent;
Therefore you see this wide domain, just as you
see your own,
Grow weaker as the distance grows the greater
from the throne!
And, therefore, in your island home, like lion in a
cage,
You lash yourself, from time to time, in self-complacent
rage!

But, Johnny Bull, my cotton friend, I think I'll
show you soon,
This country's in her morning yet, and not approached
her noon;
And though a passing cloud does now across the
horizon float,
It's in our country's glorious sun but as a passing
mote!

And when dispelled, breaks forth again, in warmer, brighter rays;
And then a wondering world will on our country's grandeur gaze;
And if the hand of Heaven should leave our 'scutcheon free from stain,
The honest heart will say 'twill ne'er look on its like again!

I'd rather be your friend, John Bull; but if you'll have it so,
Your course will leave a bitterness that I dislike to owe;
Your once respected English name will be the food for scorn,
The memory of your shameful course an ever-rankling thorn.

It may be in the course of time, some generations
hence,
May fade into oblivion the wounds of this
offence;
And, when from the Gulf unto the Lakes, our flag
floats o'er the free,
Our onward course with power and wealth is
marked from sea to sea,
Magnanimously great, we may forget your mean-
ness now,
And all we owe you in the past, with graciousness
allow!
And so, good-bye, my sometime friend; you'll find
your error out,
Before you've quite made up your mind, what you
have been about;
And then your English pride will have a quite suf-
ficient fall;
So, in pity, for the present, let us kindly drop the
pall!

THE METEOR FLAG OF ENGLAND.

THE meteor flag of England—
  Will it never float again,
A sign of promise in the sky,
  Of Freedom unto men?
When urged by giant WILBERFORCE,
  She led the nations' van,
To shield that heaven-descended right—
  The liberty of man?

The meteor flag of England
  Has waved o'er many a field
Of triumph, when the waves of steel
  From British valor reeled.
Then glowed above the carnage dire—
  A sign of battle won—
The glory of her arms so bright,
  In victory's burning sun!

The meteor flag of England
  Will turn with shame more red;
And every gallant Englishman
  In sorrow bow his head;
That English pride should e'er forget
  The glories of the past;
And to Slavery's Gorgon head
  To cringe for gold at last!

The meteor flag of England
  Was humbled on the seas,
By those who ne'er to Spanish lust
  Would bend their honest knees.
Their kindred, on this Western shore,
  Are worthy of their sires;
And in the holy cause of Right
  Will emulate their fires.

The meteor flag of England
  May meet again the foe,
That broke the prestige of her name
  In battle long ago.
The kindred blood of Marston Moor
  Has flowed at Lexington,
And built an empire round thy grave,
  Immortal WASHINGTON!

The meteor flag of England
  Will go down into the night,
That swallows up all tarnished fames,
  Like meteor from the sight;
And in the battle and the breeze,
  Shall wave o'er every sea,
That flag lit up with heavenly light—
  The standard of the free!

Pasquinades.

Is IT strange
That this poor wretch should pride him in his woe?
Take pleasure in his abjectness, and hug
The scorpion that consumes him? Is it strange
That, placed on a conspicuous throne of thorns,
Grasping an iron sceptre, and immured
Within a splendid prison, whose stern bounds
Shut him from all that's good or dear on earth,
His soul asserts not its humanity?

—SHELLEY.

KING COTTON AND KING CORN.

KING COTTON throned in regal state,
  On Carolina's sands ;
Four million slaves around him wait,
  To hear his stern commands.

"I've ruled the East, I've ruled the West,
  I've ruled the South and North ;
And empire on my crown shall rest,
  Or what's my power worth ?

" The North has tried to curb my sway,
And elevate King Corn ;
A fellow that's, all people say,
The lowest cur that's born !

" Divided power can never be
But cause of discontent."
So, in a reckless hour, he
Our country's banner rent.

Then, gathering all his ragged band,
King Cotton blew a blast,
That roused the freemen of the land,
As if a tornado passed.

King Cotton needed many things
To set his kingdom up ;
So in conclave they hit upon
A plan, o'er many a cup.

It was the good old kingly way,
  The bandit's, and the pirate's plan:
Let those keep all who have the power,
  And those steal all who can!

So, with little thieves and big thieves,
  These rascals all together,
Of Uncle Samuel's sheep and goats,
  Made a very pretty tether!

They stealéd here, and they stealéd there,
  Ah, me! what a thieving sight!
Until this vaunted chivalry
  Were ready for the fight.

Then old King Corn his banner spread
  Above his golden grain,
The type of hungry millions fed,
  And life without a stain.

And like a trumpet's clarion peal,
  He calls his millions forth,
To fight, with sturdy arms of steel,
  The battle of the North.

Then bold King Cotton's brazen cheek
  Grew quickly pale as death:
He never thought King Corn could speak
  Above his low-born breath.

King Cotton, now in wild despair,
  Called Heaven and Earth to see
That he was fighting for his share
  Of land and Liberty!

The clanking of his bondman's chains
  To this call gave the lie!
Like vampire, all their life-blood drains
  This monarch, till they die.

The world looked on with different eyes,
  To see the conflict run;
Each hoped to see the glittering prize
  By their favorite monarch won.

King Corn was worsted in the start,
  Yet flinched he never then!
But only paused to teach the art
  Of warfare to his men.

His soldiers from the ploughshare came,
  And all unused to war;
But fired by never as pure a flame
  As followed Freedom's star!

King Cotton, to his chivalrous sons,
  Said, "There's the path to glory;
But cursed be he who meanly runs,
  Or slinks back like a tory!"

Yet, strange to say, in every fight,
  This vaunted chivalry
Ran, panic-stricken, from the sight
  Of mudsill, praying Yankee!

And thus, the braggadocio crew
  Of bowie and revolver,
Soon found that oaths, and whiskey too,
  With Dixie, were all over!

And that bombastic chivalry,
  Like many an antique notion,
When storms grew high upon the sea,
  Was swallowed in its motion!

And poor King Cotton, thin and pale,
  Now falls before King Corn;
Whose golden plumage on the gale,
  His triumph shall adorn!

King Cotton in dishoner lies;
His brief dominion's o'er;
And to come in mourner's guise
Alas! there none so poor!

His fate a sign on Time's highway,
To all that come hereafter—
The jackdaw pride will sure decay,
Whatever gale may waft her.

And power built on human woe
Must of its weakness fall;
Its own oppressed will strike the blow,
And wind it in its pall.

Time, the avenger, 's always sure,
Though waiting, years grow dim:
Yet, the faithful heart can much endure,
When resting its hopes in Him!

The good and true shall always reign,
  With high, triumphant hand;
Though for a time the soil of sin
  May blister o'er the land!

All rottenness in time shall pass;
  Crimes of their own weight shall fall;
And conscience shows in shadow's glass
  The handwriting on the wall!

Now, glory be to old King Corn,
  The monarch of the land;
Who blessings from his golden horn
  Bestows with lavish hand!

Now, glory be to old King Corn,
  The monarch of the wave;
Whose flag, by foul Rebellion torn.
  Now floats above its grave!

NATURAL HISTORY OF THE LION.

THE lion, 'tis said, when in sullen mood
Is, of all beasts, most beastly rude;
Will snarl and bite at the smallest prey
That dares to intrude on his lordly way,
    As he prowls through the thicket at night;
And will only strike at an equal foe,
When he little expects to receive the blow;
    And so he has conquered in many a fight.

But, oh! when the lion is hungry, then,
Look out for a ravage in wood and glen;
For the kind of prey he does not care,
So long as he gets his glutton share;
As he slaughters with beastly will,
He lashes his tail, and a thundering roar
Is his usual way of asking for more—
Of whose, no matter—to glut his fill.

Once to the lion a name was given,
The noblest of beasts beneath the heaven;
But later travelers have found him out,
So there can be not a bit of a doubt
That he is a villainous beast at best!
Smiting the weak, and shunning the strong;
Trampling the right, and upholding the wrong;
Like a thief with his character all undressed.

Ho! ho! there's a Lion across the sea,
Who once was a champion of liberty;
And spluttered and growled at the whole wide
world,
Because Freedom's banner was not unfurled
At the nod of the Queen of the Wave;
And shake the world, like the lightning stroke
Shivers to atoms the mighty oak,
By freeing each African slave:

But, ho! ho! when the proper time came
For cleansing the earth of this wicked shame,
The lordly lion had hungry grown,
And with hunger his chivalry all had flown;
And the African slave might die,
So he got plenty of cotton to spin:
No matter how deep he dabbled in sin,
If he could but pile the guineas high.

Oh! the Lion, he is a lordly beast,
If you will only give him a glutton's feast;
But stint his maw, and you'll quickly stare
To see how his lordship will rant and rear
    At the low-bred curs, that assume
To teach him a neighborly way to live;
Play never the bully, but nobly give
    Each nation on earth its proper room!

The Lion was rampant on land and sea,
As ever a lordly lion could be;
The Russian has clipp'd his land domain;
And the West has rivaled his ocean reign;
    No wonder he growls and raves.
Who shall say but that you or me
His trident broken may live to see,
    And America rule the waves?

A WORD TO JEFF.

Oh, Jeff, my boy ! now don't you think
  Your course was very scurvy,
Because we found you out at last,
  To turn us topsy-turvy?

We know it's very hard for rogues
  To live with honest people,
Who keep a Bible in the house,
  And love a church-house steeple.

But as we kept you all in place,
  And 'lowed you to o'eride us,
We thought, in common decency,
  You might as well abide us.

Perhaps you thought that we grew rich
  A buyin' of your cotton;
And extendin' of your merchants' notes,
  Until they grew quite rotten!

And so you thought you'd "go alone,"
  Without the aid of us, sir!
And said that you would soon get up,
  With all the world. a muss, sir!

You counted on old England too,
  But a slippery boy is Johnny;
His eye is always on the chance
  Of making lots of money.

And well he knew that we had lost
  By trusting you at random ;
And so he thought he'd let you drive
  Alone your team a tandem !

Which was a very funny sight,
  To see it run the faster,
When, in mistake, you chanced to hitch
  The slave before the master!

Besides, you knew my boys were up,
  And dressed in fightin' fashion;
So Johnny very wisely crabbed,
  And 'scaped a tarnal thrashin' !

And as for all your thievin' crew,
  When we get tired of bangin'
You all to pieces, just for change,
  We'll try a hand at hangin' !

JOHN BULL SENDS A MISSIONARY TO THE AMERICAN CANNIBALS.

OH, Johnny Bull awoke one morn
  To find this Yankee nation,
About its cotton and its corn,
  Was quite beyond salvation.

And so he sent an LL. D.
  Across the Atlantic Ocean,
To write us up or down, as he
  Might suit his British notion.

But, like all Englishmen who write
About young Yankee Doodle,
His prophecies, when brought to light,
Proved him to be a noodle!

He found us cannibals at work
Each other up a eatin'!
More horribly than bloody Turk—
More foolishly than Cretin!

This ponderous indagator
Pursued ingurgitation
In scandal shops, and said the war
Would bring retrogradation.

He grew so diversiloquent,
With pen encyclopedical,
About the North's endamagement,
With reasoning polemical—

That, cock-a-whoop ingrandated,
  He nursed his ingannation,
Till Yankee Doodle tapped his head,
  And found exinanition!

But Johnny Bull, with open eyes,
  Gulped down the marvelous stories;
And whispered, looking wondrous wise,
  "He's the LL. D. for tories!"

He doffed his skin, and changed his name—
  This *whelp* from lion's lair—
And from a jobbing *bull* became
  A gambling Wall street *bear!*

THE BATTLE OF NEWBERN: OR CHIVALRY ON THE RAMPAGE.

In days of yore, when gallant knight
Donned his armor for the fight,
Expecting he his adversary,
Was ever cool and ever wary;
His prowess never did deride,
But scanned him with a warrior's pride.
But in this degenerate age,
When chivalry's on the wild rampage,

With staggering air and blustering oath
These pseudo-heroes cannot brook
To have their self-complacent sloth
By outside barbarian look
Disturbed; and all despise
The strength that in their foeman lies.

And thus they scarcely deigned to say,
They'd whip the Yankees in the fray,
Considering our fame enough,
For them to handle such mean stuff,
As Northern mudsills were made of;
Presuming that the world would grant
Unto their vaunted chivalry,
All the glory they might want,
Without stooping from their dignity.

To chase the North like flying deer,
Before the Southern cavalier;
While, like Quixote, they would sally
O'er the mountains, through the valley,

And never find, on tented field,
A foeman worthy of their shield,
But each mudsill would from them run
Like the frightened Liliputian.

In sooth, it was a splendid plan
For a blustering, lazy man;
But if you count without your host,
'Tis ten to one that you are lost.
At Newbern these bold knights sat down,
To hold till death that tarry town,
Against the paltry Yankee craft;
And o'er their cups and dice-box laughed!
Drinking punch and shuffling cards,
While came on the Yankee cowards;
And woke them up with pealing gun—
Disturbed them in their roystering fun—
And set them on heroic run!
After they found that Northern men
Could charge the breach, and charge again,

Against the cannon, with their steel,
And never from the volley reel;
Though falling 'round them, thick and fast,
Their comrades dying as they passed,
Unto the ramparts, battling still,
With steady nerve and iron will!

Now, being all most learnéd men,
As rampant with the sword as pen,
They had laid down that good old plan
Of safety to a cornered man:
"That he who fights and runs away,
May live to fight another day;
But he that is in battle slain,
Will never live to fight again!"
And as their fighting men were scarce,
Their drama ended in a farce.
In front they had their ramparts high,
Behind their baggage cut and dry;
So that, when 'gainst them went the fray,
They were prepared to run away!

Their forts were all like funnels made;
From its point their cannon played
Against the sturdy Yankee foe,
Until he mounts the rampart's brow;
With the funnel's open mouth
Shaped widely to the sunny South,
That when the dreadful Yankees come,
To run they will have ample room!

ABOUT A PIECE OF CHEESE.

Our Congressmen now are as busy as mice,
That cluster round excellent cheese;
Each prays from his soul to be spared from the vice
That crooketh all pliant knees!

But, like the ostrich, who hides his nose,
With their heads in the toothsome cheese,
They vainly think that nobody knows
How they bend *their* pliant knees!

AN OLD JOKE NEWLY VERSIFIED.

Two contractors traveling,
A gallows met their view;
"My friend, where would you be
If yon post had its due?"

"Faith," quoth the other, with a smile,
"If it had but its own,
The rest of the journey I
Would jog along alone!"

GOVERNMENT OFFICERS REPORTING TO THE PRESIDENT.

"DICK," quoth the President, "tell us what you
Have been about, or what going to do?"
"Why, the fact is," says Dick, as he opens his
eyes,
And looks at the President filled with surprise,
"Since I have been quartered in this capital,
I believe I've been doing just nothing at all!"
"Hum!" says the President, "Johnny, relate
The numberless things you have done for the
State."
Johnny looked simple, but he couldn't demur,
So he snuffled, "I've been helping my friend
Dicky, sir!"

BIBLICAL AUTHORITY FOR REBELLION.

'TIS true that foul rebellion's sword
Works the vengeance of the Lord.
As Egypt was in Bible doomed,
When clouds of locusts o'er them loomed
That ruined all their ripening grain,
And made their land a desert plain;
So, where goes Rebellion's host,
Eating away, at others' cost,
The peaceful farms and fields of green
Of all their fruit are ravaged clean.

By power divine to act they claim—
We know the locusts did the same,
Therefore, we must acknowledge it
According is to Holy Writ:
They are themselves the locust cloud,
That folds their land in famine's shroud!

THE ANACONDA.

THE Anaconda, when gorged to the full,
Lies like a log all torpid and dull;
But when digestion has done its work,
The snake for a victim doth hungry lurk.

So the Potomac Constrictor, for many a mile,
Lay torpid, and seeming indifferent the while;
Then, slowly uncoiling, till fully awake—
The South was all crushed by the folds of the snake!

MY CHIVALRY! GOOD NIGHT!

Alas! I thought I'd whip the North,
  Because he cringed so long;
I little thought he'd sally forth,
  Like giant swift and strong,
And laugh to see our puny bands
  Oppose him in the fight;
He's crushed us with his iron hands
  My chivalry! good night!

In conscious strength his people wait,
  To deal the deadly blow,
That levels down our vaunted State,
  And lays our empire low.
Oh, never more, on flood or field,
  Will we brave him in the fight;
We fall beneath his ponderous shield:
  My chivalry! good night!

THE HERCULEAN PLAN.

THE ancients, to cleanse the Augean stable,
Thought that Hercules was not able;
Nor would he have been, had his labor
Been as supposed his thoughtless neighbor,
Who from his tact experience learns;
The river's volume he quickly turns;
Away the filth of thousand years,
The bounding torrent shortly clears!
Oh! ye who cleanse the Southern land,
Work not with a rope of sand;
But try the good Herculean plan,
And sweep at once away the ban!

NURSERY RHYMES.

"WHO killed King Cotton?"
"I," says King Corn,
"One bright May morn,
And I killed King Cotton."

"Who'll toll the bell?"
"I," says John Bull,
"With grief chock-full,
And I'll toll the bell."

"Who'll dig his grave?"
"I," says the slave,
"How I'll bury the knave!
And I'll dig his grave.

THE MUDSILLS.

ALAS! that our chivalrous sword,
  And honor, so quick and keen,
By fate should be so lowered
  As to slaughter mudsills mean.

Alas! that the mudsills mean,
  With a stroke of their plebian sword,
Should pluck the jackdaws clean,
  With never a boastful word.

SAMBO'S VIEW.

OH! massa's run away;
  The Yankees comin' after;
We'll have a holiday,
  And split our sides with laughter!

If massa should come back,
  He'll find dis nigga gone,
To plant de tater track,
  And hoe dis nigga's corn!

Soldiers! you have left your calling;
    And, at sound of kettle-drum,
    From your homes and workshops come,
Where the good and true are falling!

On your arms the hour is pressing,
    With a woe of heavy weight—
    Perilled fortunes of the state—
Hearts all wrecked, so late caressing!

Oh, what harvests are you reaping!
    Glory, fame, immortal truth,
    Circle your brows, heroic youth,
Who've the nation in your keeping!

Breasting yet the sea of slaughter,
In the holiest cause that ever
Claimed manhood's best endeavor,
Your willing blood is poured like water.

In the course of time will hither
Come from every land the true,
With memories green of you,
Better than wreaths that soon will wither!

Soldiers of our hopes, adieu!
Here we lay aside the pen,
And back to busy life again,
But always breathing prayers for you!

NOTES.

NOTES.

---

(1) " *God bless the brave old Union Flag.*"
Page 23.

When the Federal gunboats ascended the Tennessee river to Alabama, the old flag of the Republic was greeted with shouts of joy by the inhabitants along the shore.

(2) *Battle of the Cumberland.*
Page 34.

Though this poem relates the fall of Fort Donelson, on the Cumberland river. it also attempts to describe the marshaling of the entire army of the Mississippi Valley.

(3) *Sigel's charge at the Battle of Pea Ridge, Arkansas.*
Page 42.

Our cavalry penetrated along the main ridge beyond the road by which the enemy had come, and were on the point of seizing some of the enemy's wagons, when a brigade of rebel cavalry and infantry attacked them. Then followed one of the most sanguinary contests that has ever been seen between cavalry. Most of the fighting was done at close quarters. Pistols and carbines having been exhausted, our sabres were brought into requisition. The rattle of steel against steel, our sabres against their muskets and cutlasses, was terrific. Nothing like it had been heard before. The rebels were Texan Rangers, and fought like demons. *The slaughter was awful, our Missouri cavalry cleaving right and left, leaving in front of their horses windrows of dead and wounded.* The enemy fell back in dismay, and our forces pursued them along the road for about a mile, when they opened a battery upon the mass of friend and foe, plowing through them with solid shot and shell. Col. OSTERHAUS had succeeded in his attempt, and retired, bringing off his dead and wounded in safety.

DEVOTION OF AN ARTILLERYMAN.—One of the most signal instances of superhuman bravery is connected with the loss of these guns. One of the cannoneers, who has long been noted for his wonderful pluck, remained at his post to the last. Placing himself in front of the piece, he disdained to save himself, but, with navy revolver, stood calmly awaiting the hooting crowd of the rebels. He emptied every barrel of his pistol, and then, with his short sword, defended his piece until he was struck down by the blows of rebels. His body was afterward found near the piece, pierced with seventeen balls, and his head cloven open with a tomahawk.—*Correspondence of the World.*

(4) *Love's Pilgrimage.*

Page 100.

They have crowned the rebellion by the perpetration of deeds scarcely known to savage warfare. The investigations of your committee have established this fact beyond controversy. The witnesses called before us were men of undoubted veracity and character. Some of them occupy high positions in the army, and others high positions in civil life, differing in political sentiments. Their evidence presents a remarkable concurrence of opinion and of judgment.

Our fellow-countrymen, heretofore sufficiently impressed by the generosity and forbearance of the government of the United States and by the barbarous character of the crusade against it, will be shocked by the statements of these unimpeached and unimpeachable witnesses, and foreign nations must, with one accord, however they have hesitated heretofore, consign to lasting odium the authors of crimes which in all their details exceed the worst excesses of the Sepoys of India.

Inhumanity to the living has been the leading trait of the rebel leaders, but it was reserved for your committee *to disclose as a concerted system their insults to the wounded and their mutilation and desecration of the gallant dead.* Our soldiers, taken prisoners in honorable battle, have been subjected to the most shameful treatment. All the considerations that inspire chivalric emotions and generous consideration for brave men have been disregarded.

It is almost beyond belief that the men fighting in such a cause as ours, and sustained by a government which, in the midst of violence and treachery, has given repeated evidences of its indulgence, should have been subjected to treatment never before resorted to by one foreign nation in a conflict with another. All the courtesies of professional and civil life seem to have been discarded. General Beauregard himself, who, on a very recent occasion, boasted that he had been controlled by human feelings, after the battle of Bull Run, coolly proposed to hold General Ricketts as a hostage for one of the murderous privateers, and the rebel surgeons disdained intercourse and communication with our own surgeons taken in honorable battle.

The outrages upon the dead will revive the recollections of the cruelties to which savage tribes subject their prisoners. They were buried in many cases naked, with their faces downward. They were left to decay in the open air, *their bones being carried off as trophies* sometimes, as the testimony proves, to be used as personal adornments, and one witness deliberately avers that the head of one of our most gallant officers was cut off by a secessionist to be turned into a drinking cup on the occasion of his marriage.

Monstrous as this revelation may appear to be, your committee have been informed that during the last two weeks the skull of a Union soldier has been exhibited in the office of the Sergeant-at-Arms of the House of Representatives, which had been converted to such a purpose, and which had been found on the person of one of the rebel prisoners taken in a recent conflict.

The testimony of Governor Sprague, of Rhode Island, is most interesting. It confirms the worst reports against the rebel soldiers, and conclusively proves that the body of one of the bravest officers in the volunteer service was burned. He does not hesitate to add that this hyena-desecration of the honored corpse was because the rebels believed it to be the body of Colonel Slocum, against whom they were infuriated for having displayed so much courage and chivalry in forcing his regiment fearlessly and bravely upon them.—*Report of Congressional Committee on the Conduct of the War.*

(5) *The Tax-payer's Song.*
Page 140.

The pirates who infest the ocean, under the commission of the rebel chief, are not more deserving the execration of mankind, than the gang who, on land, are suffered to feast upon the sweat of the poor and the blood of the brave. While the nation is straining at every nerve, and bleeding at every pore, these heartless creatures, for gain, to gratify unholy passions—wretches

" Who shrine their lusts in Heaven,
And make a pander of their God, "

have a firmer grasp upon the throat of the nation than this armed rebellion. Like panthers, at set of sun, across the nation's darkened path, they

" Bound upon their startled prey."

And while this mighty nation, this giant of the West, is trembling beneath its great weight, its arms growing weary, all its nerves and sinews quivering—almost while life is ebbing from its veins—if gold could be extracted from the quartz, they would pick by piecemeal the rock on which he stands, or if they could make merchandise of his locks, dishevelled by the rough tempest, would shear him of his strength. They follow

" With that keen second scent of death
By which the vulture snuffs the food."

If we cannot overcome the open enemy in front, let us at least banish the masked traitor in our midst. Do this, and you strengthen anew the arms and add to the courage of the nation; inspire hope, and insure the conviction that all will be well. Traitor spies have been walking your streets, feasting at your saloons, promenading at your levees, and sleeping in your capital. They have been engaged in your departments, making drawings of your fortifications, aggregations of your armies; all your consultations, your plans of battles and order of marches have been communicated to the enemy. Your generals have been paralyzed, your armies defeated, by the very men who are feeding upon the bounty of your government—betraying your confidence and the land which holds the graves of their fathers.

" Oh, for a tongue to curse the slave,
Whose treason, like a deadly blight,
Comes o'er the counsels of the brave,
And blasts them in the hour of might!"

Sir, I am not one of those disposed to question or distrust the ability or correctness of our leaders. I have always believed that a poor general, with the confidence of the people, was far better than a Napoleon or Hannibal with mutterings of complaint and half-uttered distrust. We cannot afford another defeat. Those who control our armies will ill discharge their duty if they are guided by aught else than their own matured judgments. But I have a right to insist that we shall use all the means which a God of providence has placed in our reach.

No war has been more causeless; no rebellion with so little of complaint since the angels fell; no treason which threatened so much destruction, and imperilled so much of happiness for the present, or hope for the future ; none involving so much of crime against humanity, or sin against Him who guides the destinies of nations. Men in arms were formerly our brethren ; and, while in peace we would treat them as friends, in war let us treat them as enemies. They are seeking to wrap in flames the temples which their fathers built, and in which they worshipped. They are trampling under foot the constitution and laws which their fathers ordained, and of which they boasted ; above all, they have despised and rent in twain the flowery banner which their fathers and ours planted in victory on Saratoga and Yorktown's plains—that banner which floated in triumph at Chippewa and New Orleans ; under which, on the plains of Mexico, the Palmetto regiment and the volunteers from the Empire State fought side by side, where the gallant Butler fell. They cannot divorce the American people from that noble ensign ; each stripe on its starry fold goes back and entwines itselfs around the battle-fields of the Revolution. Every star stands as a sentinel over the grave where the patriot sleeps. How deep the crime of those who have been reared to sing of its power, now to trample and despise it. Are not such men the basest of enemies, who should feel our punishments and our vengeance too? Will you talk of the constitutional rights of men who are steeped in the gall of such damning infamy? In this war, it matters not what may be their institutions. No matter though they be the best on earth, if we can harm them, punish them, subdue them, by sundering their institutions, it is our duty to do so. A rebel sells you a horse for one hundred dollars, which you agree to pay him by solemn contract, in writing ; he comes, steals the horse, and then demands that you shall pay him the price agreed. It will not do for this administration nor for us, with a half million of men sleeping on their arms, to be apologizing with proclamations which are senseless ; that we should be dancing like harlots in the antechamber of this stupendous criminal, though armed to destroy, and surrounded with the minions of an enslaved nationality. To the incendiary who puts a torch to your dwelling and is despoiling you of family and property, would you stand crouched on one knee, begging like a dog that you did not mean to burn his dwelling or destroy his property? No, sir; let us stand in the dignity of our national manhood. And he who violates our constitution, tramples on our flag, or perils our commerce, is an enemy whom we should strike, whether it be in the destruction of life or property.

Already has judgment been pronounced; it has been decreed that they should suffer death, and are now, or should be, undergoing the penalty. As well might they cry out for constitutional rights, as for the malefactor in the penitentiary, or the murderer under the gallows, to claim the rights of life, liberty, and the pursuit of happiness. Let not generals be issuing orders to degrade the manhood of our troops by rescuing or returning fugitive slaves. Let them not be exercising their talents to determine how they shall hunt slaves, rather than capture rebels. Let them not treat a loyal black man worse than a traitor master. See, just before the battle of Manassas, a general occupies part of his time in writing orders that no fugitive slaves should be allowed within the lines. Had slaves been suffered to bring intelligence and give warning, many of our brave soldiers might not now be sleeping in death on that dreadful field. He must have read the history of his own country to but little purpose, or he would have known that two of the most disastrous defeats our arms sustained in the South during the Revolution were because two slaves guided the enemy to the camps of our fathers. The slaves who periled their lives to ferry our maimed soldiers over the Potomac at Ball's Bluff you would return to chains and stripes, while you claim to protect the constitutional rights of the traitors who had wounded them. Some men among us talk of compromise and peace. None desire peace more than we. Let these men not importune us; we have not provoked nor encouraged this war. Let them go to the rebels, who stole our guns, unlimbered them, fired upon our fort, and disgraced the flag. Let them go to the men who are floating the black flag of treason almost in sight of the Capitol. Let them go to the men who make night hideous with demoniac shrieks of disunion over the grave where the bones of Washington are mouldering. Let them go to Richmond and ask the rebel crew to pull down the Confederate banner, and float the Stars and Stripes in its stead, over our custom-house and post-office.

Let them go to Charleston and New Orleans, roll themselves in sackcloth and ashes, and ask that the ensign of their fathers shall float in their ports. Let them do this, and we will have peace. We ask for no more; we will submit to no less. Let them do this, and the sword of every Northern soldier will be returned to its scabbard, and he will no longer pray to teach his hands to war and his fingers to fight. We know their terms of compromise. The traitor Davis, taking advantage of his position while here to mature his conspiracies, in the other end of this Capitol, wanted us to roll up and lay away the national flag. Roll it up, and lay it away! Why, it had been made glorious in three wars, and the wreath of its victories was yet green. It had carried American civilization over the prairies of the West; from the mouth to the source of the Father of Waters, across the great wastes beyond; from the summit of the Rocky Mountains its protecting folds covered a land washed by two oceans. Roll it up and lay it away! Why? It had floated our commerce on every sea, was the emblem of our nationality and power in every port. Its folds were stiffened by the spray of the Northern ocean, and languidly it hung to the masts in tropic seas. Roll it up and lay it away! Never. It was powerful to protect Martin Koszta thousands of miles from this Capitol, and it shall be powerful to protect the loyal citizen wherever he may be found; men like Johnson, in Eastern Tennessee; and Holt, in his Kentucky home. If this be not so, let us perish, and as a nation be forgotten; better our history had never been written; better the Declaration of Independence had never been penned; better the blood of the Revolution had never been shed.

It is no wonder that the thrones of England and France and the despotisms of Europe are in sympathy, and, as far as they dare, in action against us. They know this to be the last hope of freedom, the last home of the oppressed. They know that the great American people are in sympathy with the downtrodden, with the hewers of wood and the drawers of water, on the Eastern continent. They know that the revolutionists may wage the battle for the rights of man, and, if unsuccessful, find a city of refuge here. United, they know that we are powerful to defend our own, and protect the rights of others ; divided, our power is gone, and we become as feeble as the republics in South America. They know that the political exile, the captive in his dungeon, the soldier of liberty, whether on the summit of the Alps, or in its deep ravines, in the gloom of Hungary, or amid the desolations of Poland, are breathing forth prayers that in this great battle the rights of man may be victorious. They know, if we are divided, defeated, destroyed, the dust of centuries will longer remain upon the throne of power ; the crown will rest more easy on the despot's brow, and every tyrant grasp more firmly the sceptre which he wields. Let us disappoint them, while we frustrate the schemes of speculators counting their gains, and politicians gambling for the succession by the half-opened grave of the Republic. The dead past, from out the page of history, is looking down upon us ; the living present, throbbing with hope, trembling with fear, is looking down upon us. The on-coming future, the echo of whose millions' footfalls in the corridors of time we can almost hear, is looking upon us, beckoning to us, and in silent prayer beseeching that we may be true to ourselves, to the great legacy our fathers bequeathed, to the trust placed in our hands, to enjoy and transmit, not to tarnish and destroy. By all the memories of the past; by all the prospects of the present; by all the hopes of the future, let us rid ourselves of the sappers and miners at home; conquer this rebellion and subdue the traitors. Do you say we may not succeed ? Then let us perish in the attempt. We may vainly die for the land we cannot save ? Then be it so. Here let hope and liberty's farewell fight be fought. The pale angel of the grave can at least steer our ill-destined bark through the "Gate of Tears."

No such dreadful fate can be ours, if we are only true to humanity and the God who guides the destinies of nations, the movements of armies, as he does the sparrow in his fall. Here we make our stand ; five hundred thousand men, a wall of human hearts, to guard the land we love, the flag we honor.—*Speech of Hon. C. H. Van Wyck in the House of Representatives.*

(6) *Two or three millions of dollars a day.*

Page 146.

Eight hundred thousand strong men, in the prime of life, sober and industrious, are abstracted from the laboring population of the country to consume and be a tax upon those who remain to work. The report of the Secretary of the Treasury tells a fearful tale. Nearly two million dollars per day will hardly more than suffice to cover existing expenditures; and in one year and a half our national debt, if the war continues, will amount to the sum of $900,000,000.

This is the immense sacrifice we are making for freedom and Union; and yet it is all to be squandered on a subterfuge and a cheat? For one, I shall not vote another dollar or man for the war until it assumes a different standing, and tends directly to an anti-slavery result. Millions for freedom, but not one cent for slavery!

Sir, we cannot afford to despise the opinion of the civilized world in this matter. Our present policy narrows our cause down to an ignoble struggle for mere physical supremacy, and for this the world can have no genuine respect. Our claim of authority, based on a trivial technicality about the proper distinction between a Federal Government and a mere confederacy, amounts to nothing. The human mind has outgrown that superstitious reverence for Government of any kind which makes rebellion a crime *per se;* and right of secession or no right of secession—what the world demands to know in the case is, upon which side does the morality of the question lie? Considered as a bloody and brutal encounter between slaveholders for dominion, it is justly offensive to the enlightened and Christian sentiment of the age. Yet the fate of nations, no less than of individuals, is moulded by the actions, and these by the opinions of mankind. So that public opinion is the real sovereign after all, and no policy can be permanently successful which defies or disregards it. The human mind, wherever found, however limited in development, or rude in culture, is essentially logical; the heart, however hardened by selfishness or sin, has a chord to be touched in sympathy with suffering; and the conscience has its "still small voice," which never dies, to whisper to both heart and understanding of eternal justice. Therefore, in an age of free thought and free expression, the brain and heart and conscience of mankind are the lords who rule the rulers of the world, and no mean attribute of statesmanship is quickness to discern and promptness to interpret and improve the admonitions of this august trinity.

Sad, indeed, will it be, if those who, in this auspicious hour, are invested with the responsibility of command, shall continue to lack wisdom to comprehend, or virtue to perform their duty. This is the great opportunity which God has vouchsafed to us for our deliverance from that great curse which darkens our past. Let us not prove ourselves unequal to the destiny which it tenders. Oh! let us not attempt to rebuild our empire on foundations of sand; let us rear it on a basis of eternal granite. Let the order of justice, the harmony of God's benignant laws, pervade it. And no internal commotions or outward assaults will afterward beset it, against which it may not rise triumphant and enduring.

> "Thou vampire Slavery, own that thou art dead.
> * * * * * Yield to us
> The wealth thy spectral fingers cannot hold;
> Bless us, and so depart to lie in state,
> Embalmed thy lifeless body, and thy shade
> So clamorous now for bloody holocausts,
> Hallowed to peace by pious festivals."

Thus may the great Republic, so long perverted and paralyzed by slavery, stand forth, in the words of the Irish orator, "redeemed, regenerated, and disenthralled by the genius of universal emancipation."—*Speech of Hon. Martin F. Conway in the House of Representatives.*

(7) *Knocking them Down.*

Page 149.

* * * But slavery may be seen not only in what it has done for the rebellion of which it is the indisputable head—the fountain and life—but also in what it has inflicted upon us. There is not a community, not a family, not an individual, man, woman, or child, who does not feel its heavy, bloody hand. Why these mustering armies? Why this drum-beat in your peaceful streets? Why these gathering means of war? Why these swelling taxes? Why these unprecedented loans? Why this derangement of business? Why among us the suspension of the *habeas corpus*, and the prostration of all safeguards of freedom? Why this constant solicitude visible in all your faces? The answer is clear. Slavery is the author, the agent, the cause. The anxious hours that you pass are darkened by slavery. The *habeas corpus*, and all those safeguards of freedom which you deplore have been prostrated by slavery. The business which you have lost has been filched by slavery. The millions of money now amassed by patriotic offerings are all snatched by slavery. The taxes now wrung out of your diminished means are all consumed by slavery. And all these gathering means of war—this drum-beat in your peaceful streets—and these mustering armies—are on account of slavery and nothing else. Do the poor feel constrained to forego their customary tea, or coffee, or sugar, now burdened by increased taxation? let them pledge themselves anew against the criminal giant tax-gatherer. Does any community mourn gallant men, who, going forth joyous and proud beneath their country's flag, have been brought home cold and stiff, with its folds wrapped about them for a shroud? Let all who truly mourn the dead be aroused against slavery. Does a mother drop tears for a son in the flower of his days cut down upon the distant battle-field which he moistens with his youthful, generous blood? Let her know that slavery dealt the deadly blow which took at once his life and her peace. * * * * * * * *

The Abolitionists need no defense from me. It is to their praise—destined to fill an immortal page—that from the beginning they saw the true character of slavery and warned their country against its threatening domination. Through them the fires of liberty have been kept alive in the United States—as Hume is constrained to confess that these same fires were kept alive in England by the Puritans, whom this great historian never praised if he could help it. And yet they are charged with this rebellion. Can this be serious? Even at the beginning of the Republic the seeds of the conspiracy were planted, and in 1820, and then again in 1830, it showed itself—while nearly thirty years ago Jackson denounced it, and one of its leading spirits has recently boasted that it has been gathering head for this full time, thus—not only in its distant embryo, but in its well-attested development—antedating those Abolitionists whose prophetic patriotism is now made the apology for the crime. As well, where the prudent passenger has warned the ship's crew of the fatal lee-shore, arraign him for the wreck which has engulfed all; as well cry out that the philosopher who foresees the storm is responsible for the desolation that ensues, or that the astronomer who calculates the eclipse is the author of the darkness which covers the earth.—*Speech of Hon. Charles Sumner in the Senate.*

AS OUR BOOK IS PASSING THROUGH THE PRESS COMES NEWS OF THE GREAT VICTORIES

EAST AND WEST.

WITH victory in the East!
And victory in the West!
In glory gleams our standard now,
On Freedom's starry crest!

As falls the thunderbolt,—
As leaps the lightning's flash—
So foul Rebellion's vaunted arms
Are shattered in the crash!
With victory in the East—
And victory in the West—
In glory gleams our standard now,
On Freedom's starry crest!

To hear the cannons roar—
To see our banners soar—
Were worth a life of thousand years
Upon Elysium's shore!
With victory in the East—
And victory in the West—
In glory gleams our standard now,
On Freedom's starry crest!

When the glist'ning bayonets gleam
O'er the battle's surging stream,
The gallant hearts glide swiftly on
In Glory's splendid dream!
Oh, our eagles in the East—
And our eagles in the West—
Have led our hosts in triumph on—
The Lord our cause has blest!

Fought they gallantly and well,
As Fame's loud trump shall tell;
And shrined immortal yet shall be
Who in the battle fell.
All honored in the East—
All honored in the West—
The gallant hearts who nobly died;
Our bravest and our best!

And the standard of the free,
On the land and on the sea,
More proudly yet our haughty fence
Against the world shall be!
With victory in the East—
And victory in the West—
In glory gleams our standard now,
On Freedom's starry crest!

www.ingramcontent.com/pod-product-compliance
Lightning Source LLC
LaVergne TN
LVHW010250110826
845151LV00004B/1433

* 9 7 8 1 4 2 5 5 2 3 0 6 0 *